STRESS LESS AND LIVE AGAIN!

ELEVEN SIMPLE STEPS TO A PEACEFUL, JOYOUS FUTURE

M.A. PARKER

STRESS LESS & LIVE AGAIN

M. A. Parker

INTRODUCTION

It's not stress that kills us; it's our reaction to it. –Hans Selye

Has stress become an annoying and frustrating companion that refuses to leave? Does it feel like the walls are closing in on you, and there's no way out? Are you struggling to get through your day because of worrying thoughts? Does it feel like you have no control over what's going on in your life in general? If you are experiencing all this, chances are you are chronically stressed. Stress is something most of us experience at some point or another. However, if it refuses to go away, it becomes problematic.

Don't get further stressed knowing that you are stressed. You are not alone. Almost everyone is stressed these days due to a variety of factors. Stress affects us all, and no one is immune to it. It has become a global problem and a massive health concern.

How your body and mind respond to any demand is known as stress. It can be any type of challenge, both big and small. It could be a traumatic situation, such as losing a loved one, or something as simple as attending a job interview. Stress is triggered regardless of whether it is a big or a small challenge when it is perceived as a threat.

Everyone feels stress at some point or another in their life. Since no two individuals are truly alike, how we respond to it is quite different, too. We live in extremely stressful times. From the unexpected COVID-19 pandemic that shook our lives to a global crisis, and political instability, a variety of factors have become unexpected stressors. Financial struggles, problems in personal relationships, or unhelpful fears can also trigger stress. One thing is clear; there is no such thing as a fixed cause for the stress we experience. And therefore, it is natural that we all deal with it differently.

Even though stress is a normal physical response, it becomes problematic when left unregulated. Usually, the stress response goes away once the stressor is neutralized. However, if your body is constantly in stress-related fight-or-flight mode, it results in various health problems and complications.

No system within the body is immune to the harmful effects of stress. The effects of chronic stress are wide-reaching, from an increased risk of anxiety, depression, poor emotional regulation, risk of cardiovascular disorders, and a plethora of other problems. The answer to tackling all this is quite simple—stress management.

Perhaps you are scared of failure. Whether it is low self-esteem, unrealistic expectations, or even perfectionism, these things might be preventing you from taking risks. This, in turn, increases the stress you are already experiencing. Similarly, turning to unhealthy coping mechanisms such as substance abuse or addictions might prevent you from dealing with the stress and effectively get in the way of your relationships.

Stress can also be due to different big life decisions, such as starting a family, buying a house, or receiving an unfortunate diagnosis. These problems might require you to allocate more of your resources to them, than you are used to. This, coupled with the feeling that time is running out and the fear of missing out, further worsens stress and its repercussions.

If you are struggling with all or any of the above, understand that you are not alone. Stress has become a common occurrence in today's world, and unless you learn to deal with it, it will effectively get in the way of your life.

But don't worry, because you can tackle this! Regardless of all that you can and cannot control, how you deal with stress is one thing that's always within your control. The simple fact that you are reading this book is a step in the right direction. It shows that you are interested in learning to manage stress.

The good news is that you can easily navigate stress once you know what you should and should not be doing. This book will give you a deeper understanding of where your stress is coming from, help you to identify your stress triggers, and develop your understanding of how your existing coping mechanisms are hindering you from managing it. You will understand that asking for help is not a sign of weakness. Instead, it is a sign that you want to improve yourself. You will also learn about habits that can tackle stress and how to eliminate unhelpful habits and replace them with healthier ones. You will learn about the benefits of slowing down, improving your usual lifestyle to tackle stress, and learning to manage it. You will become mentally stronger, less stressed, and more resilient once you get through this book.

Managing your stress will improve the overall quality of your life, not just your mental health. You will feel more confident and stronger both mentally and physically; and you will feel more empowered once you manage your stress. You will learn to regain control of yourself and your life. After all, you are the writer of your destiny: Don't let manageable stress keep you from living the life you desire.

Are you wondering how I know all this? Well, I believe it is time for a little introduction. Hello, my name is M. A. Parker. Like you, I used to be chronically stressed; as recently as just a couple of years ago. I understand how over-whelming stress can be and how it affects your relationships, health, and career when left unmanaged or unaddressed. Understand that whatever you are going through doesn't have to be a permanent fixture in your life. You don't have to feel like a helpless spectator as you see your life unfold. Instead, you have the power to create the life you desire.

I remember there was a point in my life when I felt as if I was utterly helpless and powerless. I realized that it was all due to the unmanaged stress I was experiencing. After I spent countless hours researching and implementing different suggestions and advice, I realized that managing my stress was within my control.

Once I stumbled upon this realization, life became easier. You can understand your stress and where it is coming from and manage it effectively. I will show you sustainable solutions based on research and proven techniques I have tried. In this book, you will be introduced to 11 simple steps that can be practically implemented to manage your stress and live with joy and peace.

This book will act as your guide every step of the way as you learn to tackle stress. Tackling stress is possible, but it requires time, patience, commitment, and conscious effort. Once you are willing to do all this, you will become the master of your life once again. So, are you excited to get started? If yes, there is no time like the present to do it!

IS THIS STRESS?

*A*ccording to an online poll by YouGov in 2018, around 74% of individuals reported feeling so stressed they found it overwhelming or unable to cope. Some reported they over ate or ate unhealthily due to the stress they experienced, while others reported, they started to drink, increased drinking, started smoking, or increased their smoking due to stress. Similarly, some adults reported feeling anxious, depressed, and lonely because of the severity of the stress they experienced.

So, the question is: Are you stressed? If you take a moment and honestly think about how you are feeling, would you say you are stressed? Chances are you might have said you are stressed at some point or another. Stress is common, and everyone gets stressed. Trust me, even I get stressed. Stress seems to be everywhere, and most experience it regardless of age, gender, or other demographics. Before learning to deal with stress, let's understand what it means and its causes. Understanding Stress

I remember being constantly stressed. It seemed like the

walls were always closing in on me, and I had nowhere to run. The kind of stress that made me severely ill. Work certainly took its toll on my physical and mental health as well. This, coupled with eating unhealthily, dehydration, and lack of sleep, merely increased the stress I was already under.

I experienced all of this more often than I am proud to admit. There were instances when I would wake up in the middle of the night due to stress-induced dreams and puke. Initially, I wasn't sure what was causing it. I just thought something was wrong with me. It never occurred to me that the stress I was experiencing was making me sick.

The problem with stress usually starts with our inability to acknowledge its presence. Once I managed to identify that what I was going through was all related to stress, I started to work my way through it.

So, let me ask you again: Are you stressed? Maybe you need more information, and you will be in a better position to answer this question. The first thing you must understand is the meaning of stress.

What exactly is stress? It is the state of mental tension or worry caused by difficult circumstances. Stress is a natural response that prompts us to address challenges or threats. For instance, stress can propel you to work harder when you know you have an important presentation. We all experience it to a certain degree. However, our response to stress makes all the difference to our overall well-being. We all are different; therefore, differences exist in not just how we respond to stress, but in how we experience and cope with it, as well.

It is perfectly normal to feel stressed in challenging circumstances. Whether it is a conflict in our personal life or a job interview, we experience stress in such situations. For most, stress usually reduces once a challenging event or difficulty passes or when you learn to cope with it. It is time to fix this situation if you are frequently stressed or overwhelmed by it.

STRESS VS. ANXIETY

A fine line differentiates stress from anxiety. Though these words are often used interchangeably, they aren't synonyms. They are both emotional responses, but stress is often the result of an external trigger. Stress is your body's natural response to a cue sent by the brain in response to a given situation or event. On the other hand, anxiety is a psychological condition that develops when a stress response occurs repeatedly, lasts too long, and is not proportionate to the situation.

Stress can result from a short-term trigger such as a fast approaching deadline or a fight with your partner. It is a natural part of your body's fight-or-flight response. Long-term causes of stress include an inability to work or chronic illness. Stress is characterized by mental and physical symptoms such as difficulty sleeping, digestive problems, anger, irritability, tiredness, and muscle pain.

Physiologically, anxiety is similar to stress. However, it works quite differently. The feelings of uncertainty and tension are all included in anxiety. It is also associated with high blood pressure. Different situations can bring about anxiety. Anxiety becomes your body's natural response when stressed for prolonged periods. It is accompanied by fears or apprehension of all that's to come. For instance, handling your personal finances at the month's end or attending a job interview can induce severe feelings of fear and nervousness.

When these feelings become extreme and last for at least six months, it is termed anxiety.

Stress becomes your body's natural response when facing a challenging, upsetting, or uncertain situation. Some common signs of stress include a racing heartbeat, difficulty breathing, sweating, and dizziness. Anxiety, on the other hand, is usually a secondary response to stress you are already experiencing.

Anxiety is known as anxiety if a false alarm triggers your body's fight-or-flight response. Also, these responses usually outlast any situation causing the response in the first place. If you are constantly thinking about the worst-case scenario or engaging in "What-if?" thinking, worried about an uncertain future, feeling disconnected, and experiencing increased panic or dread, these are all signs of anxiety.

Even though stress and anxiety are the by-products of a similar chain of events and create similar effects, anxiety has a broader effect. Stress is often caused by external factors that are not within your control. It is often described as a physiological response triggered by your brain and nervous system. Even though anxiety is a physiological response, it also changes how you think, feel, and behave.

Anxiety is often termed an overreaction to a situation and it typically lasts for longer than proportionate to the situation at hand. Another problem with anxiety is it increases your inability to function. This is because it occurs when you struggle to properly respond or react in a situation. The indecision and feeling of overwhelm brought on by anxiety can prevent you from acting, and instead, will make you feel stuck. Stress might not always manifest as fear or dread, but anxiety almost always does. Simply put, when stress is left unregulated for prolonged periods, it can turn into anxiety.

SIGNS OF STRESS

Stress affects all aspects of your life, including your physical health, thinking ability, behaviors, and emotions. There isn't a single part of your body that's immune to stress. However, the symptoms of stress usually vary from one person to another, depending on their ability to handle it.

Some symptoms are vague and hard to describe and may be the same as once caused by other health conditions. Therefore, it's important to consult your healthcare provider when diagnosing stress. That said, here are some common signs of stress. (This list is not exhaustive by any means and just includes the common symptoms.)

- Emotionally, stress can make you feel frustrated, moody, and easily agitated. You might also experience a feeling of being overwhelmed and a dire need to take control but are unable to do so. You might struggle to relax your mind and have difficulty quieting your thoughts. You might also struggle with low self-esteem, loneliness, and feelings of worthlessness. The desire to avoid others also increases with stress.
- The physical symptoms of stress include an inability to sleep, rapid heartbeat, random headaches, stomach problems, a lack of energy, a reduction in libido, nervousness, clenching of the jaw, dry mouth, and a feeling of tingling in your

hands and feet. You might also experience random aches and pains in different muscles.

- Some cognitive symptoms of stress include forgetfulness, an inability to organize your thoughts, racing thoughts, constant worries, difficulty staying focused, poor decision-making processes, and increased negative thinking.
- Stress can also manifest as different behavioral changes, such as over or undereating, procrastination, shying away from responsibilities, and nervous behaviors such as fidgeting or pacing.

Stress causes wide-ranging symptoms. This, coupled with the fact that there aren't any specific tests available to diagnose it, makes its diagnosis doubly hard. If you are experiencing any or all of the symptoms discussed above, consult your healthcare provider immediately.

ACUTE VS. CHRONIC STRESS

The normal stress your body experiences as a reaction to a challenging or new situation is known as acute stress. Acute stress is the feeling you experience when a deadline is fast approaching or when you swerve to avoid being hit by a car. You can experience this as a response to exhilaration or joy as well. For instance, acute stress is triggered while doing something exciting such as riding a roller coaster. This short-term stress goes away relatively quickly, and your emotions should revert to their normal state.

When the stress doesn't go away for prolonged periods, then it is termed chronic stress. For instance, constant fights in a romantic relationship become a source of chronic stress.

This is the kind of stress that can seem never-ending. Those with chronic stress often struggle to see any means to improve their difficulty or change the situation that's causing their stress.

This is the kind of stress that's extremely problematic. I know because I used to be chronically stressed. Yes, I still get stressed occasionally, but I can now regulate it efficiently without it becoming chronic. My point in mentioning chronic stress is to help you understand what you are going through.

HEALTH AND STRESS

Some stress is unavoidable. That said, it is problematic if stress has become your constant companion. Stress causes wide-ranging health problems, both mental and physical. Apart from making it feel like your problems or difficulties are never-ending, it gets in the way of living how you want. In this section, let's look at the health effects of stress.

Anxiety Disorders

The inability to regulate your emotional responses in situations can manifest as an anxiety disorder, and stress can turn into anxiety if left unaddressed. The persistent fear and worry accompanying an anxiety disorder will prevent you from functioning effectively and efficiently. The high stress that comes with such conditions further magnifies the already experienced stress. It, in turn, worsens an already bad situation. It can also increase the risk of the conditions discussed below.

Burnout

Burnout is a stage at the end of the stress rainbow resulting in feelings of total exhaustion—mentally, physically, and emotionally. It is often accompanied by feelings of detachment and self-doubt. This, in turn, increases the risk of developing a negative attitude which can further increase the stress experienced.

Digestive Troubles

Digestion is one of the most common processes within the body affected by stress. Stress affects the speed with which food moves through the intestines, resulting in different digestive conditions. Some common stress-induced digestive troubles are ulcers, inflammatory bowel disease, and irritable bowel syndrome. Since stress slowly weakens the intestinal barrier, it also undermines the functioning of the immune system.

Depression

Depression is often characterized by persistent feelings of low self-worth, hopelessness, and helplessness. It can drain away your creativity, vitality, and motivation, as well. A common sign of depression is slowly losing interest in activities you once loved or enjoyed. It affects your ability to think clearly and rationally and influences your feelings and behaviors. A leading cause of depression is chronic stress.

Heart Disease

Chronic stress that is left unregulated for prolonged periods is known to increase the production of two stress inducing-hormones: cortisol and adrenaline. If their levels are left unregulated, it is known to increase the risk of cardiovascular disorders (American Heart Association, 2021). Higher blood pressure can harden the arteries. This means the heart has to work harder for optimal functioning while obtaining less than the needed supply of blood and oxygen.

Obesity

Staying in a state of constant stress is known to alter appetite. Binge eating or stress eating has become quite common. When this happens for prolonged periods, and most of the foods are unhealthy, it increases the risk of obesity. Whether it is eating too much or too little because of stress, such behaviors can result in eating disorders in the long run.

After going through this list of problems, you are likely stressed. That's ironic, isn't it? Take a deep breath and calm down. The idea is to make you aware of all you will be compromising on if your stress is left unregulated. Learning about a problem is the first step to fixing it. Now that you know how bad stress is for you, the next step is to focus on tackling it.

STEP 1: AWARENESS

If you are chronically stressed, you need to act on it. The first step to tackling stress is awareness. In general, a problem cannot be solved unless you know about it. Similarly, if you want to learn to regulate the stress you experience, the first step is to become aware that you are stressed. It all starts with acknowledging the situation at hand. To acknowledge your own situation, it is time for a little self-introspection. Here are some questions you can ask yourself to determine if you are experiencing signs of stress.

- Do you have any trouble falling asleep and staying asleep at night?
- Do you feel as if you are swamped with responsibilities?

- Do you think you don't have sufficient time to get everything done?
- Does it feel like you are crippled under an ever-increasing pile of problems?
- Do you feel exhausted with little or no time to relax?

Take some time and carefully think through these questions. Chances are, your answer will be more or less "yes" to most if not all of them. Now, don't worry, because this isn't a hurdle that cannot be overcome. If you are stressed, simply take a deep breath. The next step is to figure out what's causing your stress. From here on, you will learn a step each in the following chapters that can be used to tackle stress.

Stress isn't uncommon, and it is normal. However, how you deal with it is all that matters. You can either tackle it or let it overwhelm you. Stress is different from anxiety, and you can easily manage it with the right information.

WHY AM I STRESSED?

The American Psychological Association has been commissioning annual nationwide surveys to examine the state of stress across America to understand its impact. The results of stress in a survey undertaken in 2022 were rather alarming. It showed that most people in America are stressed, and have different stressors, too. Regardless of the demographics, stress has become a widespread and constant problem. For instance, the survey shows around 55% of Americans experience severe stress. Around 87% of participants reported that inflation and its growing prices were a source of stress for them. In that same survey, 8 in 10 Americans reported the COVID-19 pandemic as a significant stressor. Different stressors were reported, from global uncertainties to political instability within the country. There is a lot at play, from financial stressors to feeling stressed due to work or personal lives and world events.

Take a deep and calming breath. The idea of introducing these statistics is not to stress you. Instead, it shows you that there is no such thing as a single stressor. Stress can be due to anything.

If you want to tackle stress, then it is essential to understand what is causing your stress. If not, chances are you will keep getting stressed. Understanding the source of your stress or stress triggers will give you a better idea of what to do to keep it at bay.

KNOW YOUR TRIGGERS

Stress doesn't occur out of the blue. Instead, something triggers it. Just like how pulling the trigger on a gun fires the bullet, different triggers result in the onset of stress. As mentioned previously, we all experience stress due to different factors. What might stress one person might not stress others.

Identifying stress triggers is easier than explaining them. A place, thing, person, or situation that elicits an unexpected or intense emotional response is known as a trigger. Knowing that there are different causes of stress can be slightly intimidating right now. The National Institute of Mental Health (NIMH) has outlined three sources of stress triggers:

- The first type of stress trigger is routine stress.

Anything that causes stress but is a regular part of your daily life belongs to this category. Examples include heavy workloads and increased responsibilities at home.

- The second type of stress trigger is disruptive change.

Change is the only constant in life, and life is full of it. At times some changes result in excess stress. For instance, moving to a new city, getting a new job, starting a family, shifting careers, or anything else that disrupts your regular routine is a disruptive change trigger.

- The third type of stress trigger is experiencing trauma or traumatic events.

Experiencing extreme trauma, such as being in an accident, losing a loved one, or experiencing abuse are all examples of this trigger.

As you can see, there isn't a single source of stress. Instead, it can come from anywhere and at any time. The source or the stressor doesn't have to be something massive; even being overworked can be a stressor.

STAGES OF STRESS

Hans Selye, an endocrinologist, is credited with coining the term stress around 50 years ago. He came up with a stress theory that has helped us better understand what goes on in the body while stressed. He described stress as a nonspecific bodily response to any demand, regardless of whether it's caused by or a result of unpleasant or unpleasant stimuli. How you accept stress determines how you adapt to it. The general adaptation or stress syndrome hypothesized by Selye states that it is not just one change brought on by stress; it almost always manifests as a syndrome or a sum of changes.

The general stress syndrome consists of three stages. It starts in the alarm stage, moves on to the stage of resistance, and finally culminates in the exhaustion stage. In the alarm stage, your body's defensive forces are mobilized. This essentially refers to a stage where the fight-or-flight response is setting in. It is characterized by releasing hormones that increase the heart rate, blood pressure, perspiration, etc.

Your body adapts itself to the challenge in the second stage—the stage of resistance. The duration of this stage depends on the intensity of the stressor, along with your body's innate adaptation of energy reserves. Even if a machine is maintained and properly taken care of, regular wear and tear are unavoidable. Similarly, even living organisms wear out sooner or later due to constant wear and tear. However, if you are constantly exposed to the stressor, your body's ability to adapt to it also reduces.

After this, you will finally enter the third stress stage, exhaustion. This is the stage where the body has no more energy to deal with the stressor.

Stress is problematic when you cannot deal with it effectively and efficiently. It essentially gets in the way of all other functions. It is also a leading cause of different chronic health problems and conditions. Understanding the general stress response teaches you more about what goes on in your body when stressed. Learning about the stages also gives you the insight to understand what can be done to prevent stress from progressing.

IS THERE A GOOD TYPE OF STRESS?

Have you ever heard anyone say, "Oh boy, I am stressed and feel good?" Doesn't that sound funny? How can stress be good? If we don't have a little bit of good stress in our lives, we can start to feel like a rudderless ship. Also, yes, there is something known as good stress. This probably sounds silly, but it is true.

Good stress, or eustress, is the kind of stress we experience when excited. If you love riding roller coasters, you must know what this means. Your pulse starts quickening and hormones surge. However, nothing threatens or frightens you at the given moment. This stress is experienced when we receive exciting news such as a promotion. You can also experience this when doing something you were looking forward to, such as a first date. Good stress also has different triggers, and it is responsible for keeping us excited and feeling alive. This is the feeling of euphoria and excitement.

Now, the problematic sort is bad stress. This can be acute or chronic. You were introduced to what this means and the different types of it in the previous chapter. If good stress makes you feel alive, then bad stress can simply drain you out. Whether it is financial responsibilities, added personal responsibilities, or anything else happening in your professional life, bad stress can come from anywhere, and anything can cause it.

An interesting thing about bad stress is that you can usually turn it into good stress. You probably cannot do this with all your stressors, but you can certainly change your perception of a few. Understand that your body reacts quite strongly to real and perceived threats. If something isn't perceived as a threat, then the fight or flight response is not triggered. In such an instance, any fear you experience can shift to something more manageable, such as excitement or anticipation. Changing your perception about different happenings in life is possible. You will learn more about this in detail later in the book; for now, let's discuss it briefly.

For instance, instead of letting bad stress get the better of you, you can focus on the potential benefits a situation offers. After all, all clouds have a silver lining. If moving to a new city is a stressor, focusing on the good it offers, such as exploring a new place and meeting new people can make you feel better. Similarly, remind yourself of your strengths instead of focusing on weaknesses and shortcomings. Changing your mindset toward something more positive also makes it easier to tackle stress.

STEP 2: DETERMINE YOUR STRESS TRIGGERS

The second step to tackling the stress you are experiencing is to determine your stress triggers. As mentioned, without understanding your stress triggers, tackling stress is impossible. Trying to tackle stress without identifying the triggers is akin to treating an illness without knowing its cause.

The best way to identify your triggers is to think about all the different instances when you felt stressed. Grab a journal and start writing them down. After you make a list of instances, go through them and you will notice some similarities. You can also use the questions mentioned here to determine your feelings and stress triggers.

- Your boss urgently asks you to meet with them about a project you are working on. How will you feel?
- Your friend messages, "We need to talk." What are you feeling?
- Your partner asks you to help her with a household chore and you tell her you would. However, you forgot about it. How do you feel?

- It is almost the end of the month and you realize you haven't paid the credit card and other utility bills yet. How does this make you feel?
- One of your colleagues asks you to cover for them over the weekend, but you have other plans. However, you don't say "no," and scramble to get things done. How will you feel?

Visualize yourself in all the scenarios mentioned above and note how you feel. Chances are some of them will stress you out. If yes, then you have now identified your trigger! If you need more information to identify your stressors, here are a couple of other aspects you can consider.

Physical Health

A simple way to identify your stressors is by noticing your physical health. Do certain situations, places, or people make your thoughts race, your stomach drop, or your hands sweaty? This is because stress is not just a mental phenomenon but also presents a variety of physical symptoms. Becoming mindful of how your body physically responds or reacts to different situations will give you a clue about what is stressing you.

Work Life

One of the most common sources of stressors is work-related. The next time you go to work, notice how you feel when you walk through the front door, sit at your desk, or simply log on to the computer. Do the long hours fill you with dread? Do the responsibilities seem overwhelming? How does it feel if your manager or boss comes to talk to you? Noticing how you feel at work will also give better insight into any stressors present in your workspace.

Personal Life

Another common source of stress is often related to our personal lives. There can be different things that are going on that might unknowingly be causing you stress. Maybe you just purchased a new home, are going through a separation, or are someone else's primary caretaker. These responsibilities probably don't sound like much, but they are a source of significant stress.

News

And finally, flip through the news, and maybe you can identify a stressor. Stress is sometimes caused by factors beyond our purview or control. For instance, as the statistics from the survey you were introduced to previously suggest, the COVID-19 pandemic is a significant source of stress for most Americans. The pandemic is not within our control, but dealing with it is stressful.

COPING MECHANISMS—ARE THEY GOOD OR BAD?

No one has a stress-free life. We all have different types of stress, but no one is free from it. We also deal with it quite differently. I will give you an example from my own life. I remember those days when I used to be chronically stressed for different reasons. One common stressor in my life was increased responsibilities at work. I was extremely happy about climbing the corporate ladder. Still, the increased responsibilities made me feel like I had bitten off more than I could chew. Slowly, it started taking a toll on my life. Looking at how I lived, I realized I used to overeat quite a lot.

Coincidently, binge eating usually occurred right after I experienced stress or was overwhelmed for some reason. Whether it was a box of cookies or a tub of ice cream, I would just eat through it in a couple of minutes. Now I know what I didn't know then. Perhaps I knew what it was, but never acknowledged or accepted it. I used eating as a coping mechanism. Whenever I ate something sweet, I used to feel a little better. After a while, I got habituated to it. So, whenever

I was slightly stressed, I would automatically reach for something sweet. Eventually, it took a toll on my overall health and sense of well-being.

My point in telling you this little story is that we all have coping mechanisms. We use them to deal with the stress we experience. Not all coping mechanisms are helpful, and some are extremely problematic. In this chapter, you will learn more about coping mechanisms and how to develop healthy ones to deal with stress.

WHAT IS A COPING MECHANISM?

At times, life unfolds just like a movie. No, I don't mean that camera crews surround us, that we have a stylist who ensures we are well-dressed at all times, or that we have writers that tell us what our next step is. (Though all of this would be quite nice to a certain extent, this is not what I mean.) All movies have conflicts and climaxes. Similarly, life throws different conflicts our way. We all experience highs and lows. How we handle the difficult moments in life is what makes all the difference. This is where coping mechanisms step into the picture.

You might know what coping means, but understanding the definition of a coping mechanism is important. Any cognitive or behavioral approach used for managing internal and external stressors is known as a coping mechanism. To better understand what coping mechanisms mean, let's divide them into two parts. The first part consists of stressors, and the second is the approach used to deal with them.

Stressors

As mentioned previously, all stress is not the same. Though the response it elicits is the same, stressors can come from different sources. The two primary categories of stressors are internal stressors and external stressors.

Any thoughts or emotions stemming from within us and inducing our stress response are internal stressors. Common examples include catastrophizing, fear of failure, insecurities, perfectionism, and negative self-talk. On the other hand, if you experience a stress response because of factors from the outside, including people and situations that you have no control over, they are known as external stressors. For instance, an accident, losing a loved one, giving an important presentation, losing your job, and so on are all external stressors.

Approach Used to Cope

The mechanisms used to cope with stressors are as varied as the stressors themselves. Usually, coping with stress is characterized by cognitive and behavioral approaches. The best way to understand what this means is to use an example.

David missed his child's graduation day because he was incredibly busy with work and got caught up. He circled this date on his calendar and set reminders for the same for months. However, he got so caught up with an extremely important meeting that he couldn't leave on time. By the time he left, there was so much traffic that he could not make it to his child's graduation on time. When he reached the event, he realized that his child was visibly upset. This, in turn, made him feel quite disappointed in himself for letting them down. Unfortunately, as hard as he tried, he could not return and make things right. Now, what would he do to cope with this situation? Whatever he does next is his coping mechanism.

Any approach you decide to use to cope with stress related to your thinking is known as a cognitive approach.

This is one of the reasons why most of us indulge in negative self-talk in such situations. In the previous example, if David started thinking, *I always disappoint my child*, or *I'm such a horrible parent*, it would make him feel worse than he already did. Even though such thoughts aren't helpful, it is a cognitive approach he uses to deal with stress.

Similarly, we have certain approaches that help us cope with stress through our actions or behaviors. Again, let's go back to the previous example. If he apologizes to his child right away and asks what he could do to make things better and then does it, it is a behavioral approach to dealing with stress. Behavioral coping strategies include how some people reach for cigarettes or alcohol when stressed.

TYPES OF COPING MECHANISMS

Regardless of how resilient you are, eliminating all stressors is impossible. However, learning to deal with them healthily is well within your control. In this section, let's look at different techniques and the common coping mechanisms most people use.

Common Techniques Used

Coping techniques essentially refer to coping mechanisms that enable us to tackle our stressors. These techniques can be problem-oriented or emotion-oriented.

Problem-Oriented

A problem-oriented coping technique is any actionable way to tackle a stressful situation. This is quite similar to the behavioral approach you were introduced to previously. This is a great way to deal with a stressor because it encourages you to tackle the problem. Usually, you can employ this technique when you have little control over the situation. For instance, if you struggle to balance your personal and professional lives, talking to your employer about a healthier and more flexible work schedule will help solve the problem. Similarly, if responsibilities overwhelm you, you can create a to-do list that encourages you to tackle the most important and urgent responsibilities. So, dealing with the stressor becomes easy by focusing on all the things you can control, including your actions.

Emotion-Oriented

Another coping technique used is based on your emotions. It's about managing your feelings in a stressful situation. This is quite similar to the cognitive approach discussed in the previous section. It enables you to focus on yourself and your emotions triggered in a specific situation. This can be used for all types of stressors, including situations where you have very little or no control. For instance, you might get stressed when you argue with your partner. Instead of giving in to your emotions and worsening the situation, you can try journaling your feelings. Similarly, taking the time to process your grief is better than getting emotionally overwhelmed if you have recently lost a loved one. Whether it is talking to a mental health practitioner, engaging in meditation, or any other healthy technique that helps process your grief, this is the only way to deal with the stress and pain of losing a loved one.

Common Styles Used

How do you deal with a problem or a challenge? Do you try to avoid it for as long as possible until it can no longer be avoided? Or do you think you should tackle it head-on? Your answer might be different in different situations. Some like tackling their problems head-on, while others try to avoid the situation altogether. There is no such thing as a correct method to deal with all the stressors you experience, and this is where coping styles step into the picture. The two primary styles of coping are active coping and avoidant coping.

Active

When you decide to face a stressor head-on, it is known as active coping. Whether you are trying to solve a problem or are focused on how you feel about a situation, this style enables you to try and cope with a stressor to reduce its hold on you.

Avoidant

Avoidant coping is pretty much what it sounds like. It is avoidant coping if you are avoiding situations that trigger your stress response or ignoring how you feel about the stressor. Avoidant coping mechanisms are incredibly harmful because they do not solve the problem, but instead let it fester.

This reminds me of the so-called laundry chair I have in my bedroom. Most of us have a chair, couch, or spot on the floor similar to my "laundry chair." This is where we keep all random items until we need to deal with them. For me, the laundry chair is the place where I keep all my freshly washed clothes. I fold them, but I do not put them away. After a while, the entire chair is piled high with clothes that need to be put away. I keep doing this until there is no space left. Similarly, avoidant coping mechanisms do not make your problems go away. Eventually, these coping mechanisms become a source of more stress.

IS YOUR COPING MECHANISM HELPING YOU?

Until now, you were introduced to what coping mechanisms mean by different approaches, techniques, and styles associated with them. Now, as you can see from the example you were introduced to in the previous section, coping mechanisms are not always good. Some are healthy, while others aren't. Suppose you really want to tackle the stress you are experiencing. In that case, it's important to become aware of your coping mechanisms and change them if they are not serving you.

In life, a lot of situations are outside our realm of control. While struggling with a challenge or stressor, one thing that is still in your control is your behavior. You can determine how you respond to the stress you're experiencing. Healthy coping occurs when you utilize a strategy to respond calmly and rationally to the situation. Even if engaging in such coping mechanisms doesn't gratify you immediately, it makes a significant difference in the long run. It reduces stress and helps deal with challenges. So, what do healthy coping mechanisms look like? Here are a few examples to consider.

- Sharing your problems with a loved one.
- Eating healthily and exercising daily.
- Using self-calming techniques such as journaling or meditation.
- Focusing on utilizing your problem-solving skills to tackle the situation.
- Reaching out to a therapist or counselor for a little extra assistance.

If healthy coping mechanisms are on one end of the spectrum, the unhealthy ones are on the other. As mentioned, healthy coping mechanisms might not offer instant gratification, but they help. On the other hand, unhealthy coping mechanisms usually offer instant gratification. This is the only reason why most of us engage in them. However, the comfort they offer instantaneously results in a buildup of negative consequences later. Here are some examples of unhealthy coping mechanisms.

- Avoiding a challenge or a problem.
- Procrastinating and doing everything other than what you were supposed to be doing.
- Drinking excessively or indulging in drug usage.
- Eating too much or not eating enough.
- Sleeping too much or staying up all night.
- Isolating and withdrawing from social situations.
- Entertaining thoughts of self-harm.

Note: If you are entertaining any thoughts of self-harm, please immediately reach out to a mental health professional or healthcare provider!

STEP 3: YOUR COPING MECHANISMS

The next step for dealing with chronic stress is understanding your coping mechanisms. By now, you know what a coping mechanism is. Now, it is time for a little self-introspection. You cannot develop healthy coping mechanisms unless you know how to cope with stress right now. Here are some questions that will make you more aware of your coping mechanisms.

- How do you unwind at the end of a stressful day?
- What is the first thought that comes up when dealing with a stressful situation?

- Do you give in to your emotions when stressed?

Take the time needed to introspect and honestly answer these questions. Chances are you aren't coping too well with stress right now. Well, don't worry, and stop getting further stressed. Learning helpful coping mechanisms and practicing them is possible. It requires a little conscious effort and self-awareness. For instance, getting angry or upset when stressed and throwing a temper tantrum is an unhealthy coping mechanism. Similarly, other unhealthy coping mechanisms include drinking alcohol, smoking, engaging in negative self-talk, catastrophizing, and overeating. You can develop healthier coping mechanisms by following the simple suggestions given here.

The next time you feel stressed, simply leave the room. Being physically away from stressful situations is a great way to calm your body and mind. You can distract your mind instead of getting overwhelmed by putting some distance between you and the overwhelming sensations. Whether it is a quick bathroom break, a walk around the block, or even going to the next room, go ahead and do it.

When stressed, redirect the nervous energy to get some cleaning done. Whether you are reorganizing your work desk, closet, or anything else on your to-do list associated with cleaning, do it. Ensure you do not spend more than 15 minutes doing it. So, ensure it is a small task you know you can complete. By the end of this break, you will be productive and will feel better, too. This is because physical clutter can also be a source of mental clutter. Getting rid of one makes it easier to deal with the other.

You start breathing rapidly and shallowly when stressed. A simple way to rectify this is by focusing on regulating and normalizing your breathing. Shift all your attention to the simple act of breathing in and out. You can perform this exercise anywhere and at any time. So, when you feel stress coming on, close your eyes and redirect all your attention to your breath. Breathe in slowly and deeply through your nose and slowly breathe out of your mouth. Even if thoughts come, simply let them be. Concentrate only on your breathing and nothing else. Do this until you feel a little calmer.

Another great way to deal with stress instead of giving in to unhealthy coping mechanisms is journaling. Grab a pen and paper and start writing whatever you think and feel right now. It doesn't have to make any sense. Do not judge or criticize yourself for what you have written. Simply write. Think of it as a mental and emotional dump. Once you get all your thoughts out, it becomes easier to regulate them. This, in turn, reduces stress.

If stress is causing negative thinking and self-doubt, a simple way to tackle it is by shifting to a mindset of gratitude. Take a couple of moments for yourself and think about all the things you are grateful for. This ensures you are not getting stuck in negativity and instead can focus on the good you have. By focusing on all you are grateful for, you automatically welcome more positivity into your life.

If you are feeling overwhelmed, consider talking to someone about it. Whether it is a friend, family member, or a loved one, simply call and talk to them. By sharing the thoughts and emotions that are stressing you out, you can make sense of them. At times, simply saying things out loud reduces the stress you are experiencing. Even if the other person cannot help you in any way, at least they can reduce your burden by listening.

Learning to regulate stress is a perfectly achievable goal. With a little conscious effort and self-awareness, you can understand what's causing your stress. This also gives you a chance to reconsider whether your coping mechanisms are helping you or not. Also, understand that you are not alone. Even if it feels like this right now, you aren't. You simply need to learn to ask for the help you need. Read on to learn more!

IT'S OKAY TO ASK FOR HELP

*W*hether you are having a rough time at work or grieving the loss of a loved one, having supportive people is important. A reliable support network isn't just useful in emergencies, but it's also important for your overall mental well-being. The simple fact of knowing that you have others to depend on and they are there to support you itself is reassuring enough to get through a stressful situation.

Social support is known to increase resilience, too. For instance, imagine you just interacted with an unpleasant colleague at work who left you feeling defensive and stressed. You will feel better if you receive kind words or any validation from a friendly co-worker. A show of support makes it easier to relax and emotionally recover from the previous encounter. This is precisely how a social support system works.

Apart from stress relief, maintaining a good social support system helps improve your mood, promotes cognitive functioning, reduces loneliness, makes you feel under-stood, reinforces healthy habits, and adds some meaning to your life. It will also offer new perspectives and advice that can assist in problem-solving. A combination of all these aspects automatically improves your mental and emotional well-being. Since mental and physical health are related, in a way, social support is needed for your overall health.

IS IT UNDER YOUR CONTROL?

In the previous chapter, you were introduced to the concept of coping mechanisms. These mechanisms are our inherent responses to any stress we are experiencing. When it comes to stress, it plays a crucial role in an increased risk of addiction, its maintenance, relapses, and failure of treatment. When stressful occurrences are combined with unhelpful and poor coping skills, the risk of addiction automatically increases (Sinha R, 2008). This stems from impulsive responses and self-medication. Since stress cannot be fully eliminated, learning to manage it is needed.

There can be days when having a stiff drink at the end of them makes you feel better. However, if you are trying to find the solution to your stress at the bottom of a bottle, it will do you no favors. In fact, using any stimulants merely increases the stress you are already under. A drink or two can quickly turn into a weekend bender when left unregulated.

Similarly, occasional or recreational drug use can become a fixed pattern and habit. Unfortunately, the problem is a self-fueling cycle of stress and dependence. The substances mentioned above are addictive. If they are viewed as a means to stress management, you will start looking for them when stressed. Once addiction takes a stronghold, shaking it off isn't easy. This further worsens the stress you might be experiencing. In the end, no good comes out of using any addictive substances as a means to manage stress. Apart from harming your physical, emotional, and mental well-being, regular substance use, dependence, and addiction will get in the way of your life.

The link between chronic stress and internal motivation to use addictive substances is solid. The risk of addiction also increases due to adverse childhood experiences, including parental neglect, family dysfunction, and abuse. Similarly, unhappy marriages, lack of employment satisfaction, or harassment in any aspect of life also increase the risk of addiction. In a way, the greater the number of stressors anyone is exposed to, the greater the likelihood of addiction. It essentially puts us at a cumulative disadvantage over a period because the stress is left unaddressed, and addiction becomes a new problem. Using drugs or self-medication to cope with stressors might temporarily relieve the symptoms of anxiety and stress, but eventually, it results in psychological distress.

So, the question you really need to answer for yourself is whether your stress is under control or not. If you know you are engaging in unhealthy behaviors or using unhelpful coping mechanisms, there is no time like the present to break free of them. You have the power to regulate the stress you are experiencing. If you are struggling, then reaching out and asking for the help you need is important.

IS IT AFFECTING OTHERS AROUND YOU?

If you are still wondering whether you need help tackling stress, consider if it is affecting those around you. Human beings are not solitary creatures. We thrive in groups. We have different relationships that cater to our need for belonging. However, our usual behaviors affect others around us. Likewise, we are affected by those around us. If your stress is affecting others around you, it is a sign that you need help.

Even the strongest of relationships cannot last when substance abuse is thrown into the mix. Having a partner who drinks more than they should or uses drugs is similar to throwing a stone into a still-water body. It causes ripples that influence everything. Having a partner who uses alcohol or drugs to deal with their stress influences all those related to them.

Here is a hypothetical situation to consider. A dysfunctional environment is created at home when one of the partners regularly drinks too much or uses drugs. If one of the partners regularly lashes out at the other and throws fits of rage due to their substance abuse, that relationship is unhealthy. If there are children in that household, they will be exposed to chronic stress from a young age. They can develop into adults with severe anxiety or any other stress-related disorder. As mentioned, humans thrive in groups. However, any unhelpful behavior displayed by one member of the group is bound to influence all of the others in the group, too.

Any unhealthy coping mechanism or unmanaged stress is bound to get in the way of your relationships. If you notice that your stress is affecting those around you, it is a clear sign that you need help. With a little self-introspection, you can see whether unhelpful coping mechanisms are harming your relationships. With self-awareness, it becomes easier to talk about any problems or challenges you are facing right now. In the next section, you will learn how to reach out to others and ask for help.

IT'S OKAY TO ASK FOR HELP

Even though stress has become an unavoidable part of normal life, too much of it harms your emotional and physical well-being. It's rather alarming that an increasing percentage of the global population is stressed most of the time, and that it affects their day-to-day functioning. An important factor that helps deal with difficulties is an emotional support system. When you have social support, your ability to deal with stress and the resilience needed to get through it increases. Loneliness is associated with low-quality social relationships and the lack of social networks. It's incredibly easy to reach out and seek the support you need to tackle stress by nurturing supportive relationships.

Social and emotional support is helpful. A strong social support system improves your sense of autonomy and self-esteem. You don't need a massive network of family or friends to benefit from social support; even just a handful of people is sufficient. Whether it is your co-workers, neighbors, friends, family members, or acquaintances, as long as you know you can count on them, that's sufficient.

If you are aware of the stress you are experiencing, and it is preventing you from leading a happy life, it's time to reach out. A common mistake most make is we believe that we have to tackle all our problems by ourselves. We are not singular entities and cannot exist in isolation. Instead, we need a support system. However, you should also learn to reach out to them. If you don't state what you need, others will not know. Here are a couple of simple tips you can use while reaching out to others for help.

- You need to cast a wide net to grow your support network.

Social support comes in different forms, and there is no such thing as a one-size-fits-all approach. You don't have to share your problems with everyone. Do it only with those you are comfortable with. For instance, perhaps talking to a colleague at work about any work pressure you are experiencing is helpful. Similarly, you can talk to a neighbor about any household difficulties you are facing. Depending on the kind of support you need, choose a person accordingly.

- If you really want help, then you need to be proactive.

Do not wait for others to come and offer help. If you keep waiting to do this, you will never get the desired help. Instead, simply be proactive, take the first step, and reach out. What is the worst that will happen? They might not be able to help you. That's not bad, is it? Understand that asking for help is a sign of self-confidence, awareness, and self-esteem. It simply reminds us that we cannot do everything by ourselves. We need a little support, and that's perfectly okay.

If you are struggling with a specific stressful situation and know your existing social support network cannot cater to that need, you need to seek peer support. Joining support groups or attending group workshops is a great way to meet others who are sailing in the same boat as you. Knowing you are not the only one dealing with a specific problem automatically makes you feel better. This, in turn, reduces the sense of loneliness.

STEP 4: ASK FOR HELP

We all deal with stress differently. That said, it does affect our lives at one point or another. When something is worrying us, and the stress becomes overwhelming, most of us tend to bottle it up. Unfortunately, this is one of the worst ways to deal with the stress you are experiencing. In such situations, all you need to do is simply reach out and ask for help. Remember, a problem shared is a problem halved. At times, you will simply feel better by sharing your problems. If you are still wondering whether you should ask for help to deal with stress, answer the following questions.

- Do you think you are able to manage your stress?
- Is stress straining your relationships?
- Do you find yourself engaging in negative self-talk more often?
- Do you feel overwhelmed most of the time?

Once again, give yourself a time out, and focus on self-introspection. Take all the time you need and answer the questions mentioned above. If by the end of it you realize you are struggling, it is time to take action. Now that you know the problem and cannot deal with it, ask for help. If you normally hesitate to ask for help, use the suggestions given here to make it easier.

It becomes easier to ask for help when you realize you need it. The first step is always acceptance. This means you must become self-aware to understand that you are unable to deal with the stress by yourself. Even the best of us can feel flustered to the extent that we cannot function. In such situations, obtaining a little support from others helps. So, simply accept that you need help if you are struggling.

Most of us struggle to ask for help because we believe we are supposed to do everything by ourselves. Unfortunately, this is not practically possible. Humans cannot survive like islands. We require support and assistance. Forget about the stigma associated with asking for help. The simple act of reaching out to others takes a lot of self-awareness and confidence. Understand that you do not become less powerful by reaching out.

If you are considering therapy or counseling to deal with chronic stress and are doing it for the first time, visualize the outcome you desire. Perhaps you desire practical advice. Perhaps you simply want to be heard, or want to learn emotional regulation; whatever your desired outcome is, make a note of it. Once you know what you can gain by reaching out, focus on the outcome. This makes it easier to take the first step and seek the help you need.

Once you follow the advice given here, obtaining the help you need becomes easier. You should also keep yourself open to receiving help from others. There may be plenty of people around you who want to help, but if you are unable to accept it, no one can do anything. Instead, keep an open mind and accept the support you receive.

Asking for help can get you through any challenges you

are facing. It will also lessen your burdens and make it easier to keep moving. With a little help, you can easily manage the stress you are experiencing. If you want to tackle the stress you are dealing with, it is time to look within and discover the habits holding you back, like not asking for help. By breaking free of bad habits and developing new ones, you can conquer any challenge, including stress.

FOCUS ON THE NEW

*R*eaching for a cup of coffee after waking up or brushing your teeth before going to bed are examples of habits. We all have different habits. In fact, it is said that most of the actions or behaviors we engage in daily are habits. All of the things you do with little or no conscious thought, as if you are on autopilot, are habits. So, your habits ultimately decide the quality of your life. From dealing with stress to achieving the goals you want, the outcomes boil down to your habits.

This brings to mind a popular quote by Steven Pressfield: "The difference between an amateur and a professional is in their habits. An amateur has amateur habits. A professional has professional habits. We can never free ourselves from habit. But we can replace bad habits with good ones." You not only have the power to develop healthy and beneficial new habits but can break free from the shackles of the ones holding you back, too.

WHAT ARE HABITS?

We all have different habits, but do you know what they mean? Any action or behavior you engage in regularly and do automatically is a habit. Some are known to improve your physical and mental health, while others harm them in one way or the other. Understand that habits are not the same as routines. Habits occur with little or no conscious thought, whereas routines require intention and discipline. For instance, it can be a habit whenever you are stressed and start scrolling mindlessly through social media. On the other hand, if you consciously decide to warm up and cool down after working out, it is a routine.

Habits can be both good and bad. When you are doing something on autopilot, it becomes a habit. Every habit, both good and bad, offers some benefit to you. For instance, reaching for a cigarette when stressed is a habit. Similarly, washing your hands before eating is also a habit. It is entirely up to you whether the habits you are engaging in are doing you any good or not.

Whenever you do something repeatedly, it sticks. This is why habits are effortless and automatic. The benefit of a habit is it often motivates you to repeat the said behavior. Habits are extremely beneficial. For instance, developing a new habit can become a source of pride because you will realize that the power to change your life lies in your hands. This, in turn, will bring you a step closer to your goals.

Similarly, habits can also generate a sense of achievement and empowerment. For instance, if you get into the habit of exercising regularly, it will improve your physical and mental health. When you see the benefits for yourself, you will feel better and more in control. Positive habits improve your self-esteem, reduce stress, and tackle anxiety.

The terms coping mechanisms, habits, and routines are often used interchangeably. But they aren't the same. Coping mechanisms are compulsions we engage in when dealing with a stressor. On the other hand, habits are usually developed over time, stemming from the belief that they help a specific situation. Habits usually don't have anything to do with your emotional state.

In contrast, coping mechanisms are almost always related to how we feel. For instance, smoking when stressed is a coping mechanism and a habit. Let's see how. Stress can bring about a variety of unpleasant emotions. The act of smoking might help deal with those emotions. It has become a habit because the brain sees it as a more pleasurable activity than dealing with stress. When left unregulated, such habits become detrimental to your overall sense of well-being. Also, unhelpful coping mechanisms and habits prevent you from dealing with the stress you are experiencing.

CREATING NEW HABITS VS. BREAKING BAD HABITS

Habits are important. However, all habits are not helpful, and some are detrimental to your overall productivity, efficiency, and health. If you have been struggling with breaking any bad habits or want to develop new ones, there's no time like the present to do it. If you can develop a habit, then you certainly have the power to change it!

Before you learn to change an existing habit, it's important to understand what causes it. Without understanding its cause, whatever habit you develop will not stick. If there are any bad or unhelpful habits you want to break free of, start by identifying their cause.

Usually, the two common causes of bad habits include stress and boredom. It is simply our internal mechanism to deal with the stress or boredom we are experiencing. Whether it is nail-biting, impromptu shopping sprees, drinking on weekends, or even mindlessly browsing through the internet, these habits are the causes of stress or boredom.

Well, I know that you can change it. It doesn't have to be this way. You can slowly teach yourself healthier and better ways to deal with the stress you are experiencing. This, in turn, can be used to substitute any existing unhelpful habits.

At times, the stress or boredom you are actually experiencing can be a symptom of a deeper issue. For instance, you might know you are stressed. However, if you take a closer look, you might realize it stems from an unresolved personal issue. Unless that issue is resolved, the stress will not go away. Therefore, always start with self-introspection and be honest. After all, if you are not honest with yourself, how can you make positive changes? By recognizing the causes of your bad habits, it becomes easier to overcome them. You can use the tips and suggestions in previous chapters to do this.

CAN BAD HABITS BE ELIMINATED?

A common question about unhelpful habits is whether they can be eliminated or not. Honestly, you cannot eliminate a habit. Instead, you can replace it. Whether it is a good or a bad habit, these behaviors benefit you in some way or another. This is one of the reasons why we end up holding on to them. For instance, smokers usually say they feel better after lighting a cigarette. Similarly, staying in a relationship you know is bad for you is also a coping mechanism that offers emotional benefits in some way. Bad habits, as mentioned, can be mechanisms to deal with the stress you're experiencing.

The so-called benefits a habit offers can extend to smaller habits as well. Whether it is waking up in the morning and quickly checking social media or browsing mindlessly through it while working, these things can make you feel more connected. However, spending more time doing this reduces your productivity and divides your attention. It can soon become a source of stress, too. Since the tasks mentioned above make you feel as if you are not missing out, you might do them again. In fact, you will do them again. This is how bad habits take root.

Since bad habits offer some perceived benefit, eliminating them is difficult. This is one of the reasons any advice such as "simply don't do it" or "stop doing it" seldom works. So, bad habits cannot be eliminated? Now what? The answer is to replace the existing habits with something more desirable. It is about replacing the habit with another that offers a similar benefit. For instance, if you are used to smoking whenever stressed, simply stopping is not a good idea. Instead, it is better to devise a healthier way to deal with stress so you do not feel the urge to smoke. As already mentioned, bad habits usually address some needs in our lives. This is why the behavior you decide to replace the bad habit with must address the said need. If not, sooner or later, the bad habit will come back.

BREAKING BAD HABITS

Here are a couple of practical suggestions you can use to break bad habits.

The first thing you must do is find a substitute for the habit you want to break. This means you must have a plan for the next time you feel stressed. For instance, if you usually spend a couple of minutes mindlessly scrolling through social media when stressed, what can you do the next time this happens? Instead of scrolling through social media, you can perhaps go for a brief walk. Similarly, the next time you feel the urge to smoke when stressed, consider doing some breathing exercises. Once you have a plan in place, dealing with the bad habit becomes easier.

Every habit has certain triggers. By eliminating as many triggers as you possibly can, it becomes easier to change your habits. For instance, if you are used to eating junk food when stressed, getting rid of all of the junk food in your house makes sense—out of sight and out of mind. Similarly, if you feel the urge to smoke while drinking, avoiding places where you might be drinking is better. What does this mean? It essentially means by changing the environment that fuels your bad habits; it becomes easier to replace them with better ones.

Find an accountability buddy for yourself. Simply join forces, whether it is a friend, acquaintance, family member, or anyone else. You will increase your sense of accountability by telling them what you are trying to do. Our willingness to do something increases when we know someone else expects it from us. By finding an accountability buddy, it becomes easier to make a change. The added sense of accountability also acts as a motivator that pushes you to do better.

A simple way to motivate yourself to not indulge in a bad habit is by visualizing the outcome you desire. Visualize yourself succeeding, and it will make you feel better. Whatever bad habit you are trying to break, imagine yourself crushing it and then enjoying your success. Hold on to this feel-good emotion, which will motivate you to do it.

Another simple technique is understanding that you do not have to become a new person to overcome bad habits. Instead, you simply need to go back to your old self. The bad habits you are trying to break weren't always there. You might have developed them at some point. Now, the idea is to return to the previous version of yourself. If you want to stop smoking because of stress, you simply need to go back to that stage in life when you were a non-smoker. Since you could do it once, you can also do it now.

Another important aspect of tackling bad habits is to change your negative self-talk. It is easy to judge yourself when you don't act any better. Whenever you make a mistake or slip up, or engage in something you weren't supposed to, it's easy to criticize yourself. A simple way to change this criticism is by using "but." Let's assume that it feels like you are failing. Instead of thinking, *I am a failure, and I will never succeed*, replace it with, *I am a failure, but I know I can do better*, or *I am a failure, but everyone fails at some point or another*. By rewiring your negative self-talk, it becomes easier to change. You will learn more about rectifying negative self-talk in the next chapter.

Practice self-compassion and forgiveness. Understand that progress is impossible without setbacks and challenges. So, prepare to fail, too. It is okay to slip up and do something you weren't supposed to. Instead of beating yourself up for it, it is better to focus on what can be done in the future to prevent relapses. Instead of engaging in self-criticism, show a little compassion. Forgive yourself and learn to move on. Plan for what you can do if you slip up or make mistakes. If all this happens, then you will know what to do instead of getting bogged down.

1% BETTER EACH DAY

Whenever you need to change something, looking at all that's to be done can be overwhelming. Instead, focus on continuous improvement. This means you need to make small changes or improvements daily. These small improvements will add up to something significant. This is a great method to focus on self-improvement.

A common reason why most of us fail to chase a big goal is that we believe we need to make big leaps to achieve it as quickly as possible. It sounds perfect on paper but increases the chances of burnout, failure, and frustration. Instead, you can ultimately achieve the big goal by focusing on continuous improvement.

HOW DOES CONTINUOUS IMPROVEMENT WORK?

Most of us have, unfortunately, convinced ourselves that change is meaningful only with large and visible outcomes. Whether it is weight loss, success in a profession, or anything else, we believe that it doesn't matter unless the improvement is Earth-shattering, it doesn't matter. Making small changes daily is a great way to achieve a bigger result. Even if the change isn't noticeable, it eventually adds up. This is the power of tiny gains.

All you need to do is focus on being 1% better every day

than you were the day before. Initially, it was just 1%. By the end of the year, it results in a massive 37% change. Instead of achieving the year-end goal right at the beginning, focus on making a 1% change. The small improvements suddenly create a big gap or change as time passes.

TOOLS FOR CONTINUOUS IMPROVEMENT

So, how do you make a 1% change daily? Here are a couple of practices you can focus on to make continuous improvement a part of your daily life.

First, you must focus on doing more of what you know works. Even performing a fundamental task daily and doing it to the best of your abilities offers profound results. Whether it is focusing on gratitude, never missing a work-out, or simply meditating, the progress you make later will be significant.

Another thing to remember is that improvement is not just about doing more things right but reducing the wrongs, too. Instead of simply exercising daily, you can concentrate on ensuring you miss fewer workouts. Eventually, the result will be the same. However, by avoiding tiny losses, the progress you make increases.

While making a change, your attitude matters. You can either look at all the things left to be done or the ones you have completed. This means measuring your progress backward. It also means you need to decide based on what's happened instead of what you want to happen. For instance, if you have managed to stick to your weekly exercise schedule, the next goal can be to exercise for 10 days at a stretch. By focusing on gradual yet continuous improvement, you can achieve significant results.

STEP 5: FOCUS ON BUILDING NEW HABITS

Habits account for a significant amount of our daily behaviors. Apart from overcoming bad habits, you can develop new ones, too. Doing this is needed to improve your well-being, tackle stress, and work toward happiness. If you are looking to develop new habits, here are some tips you can follow.

Start Small

A common reason most people fail to develop healthy or new habits is that the task can seem overwhelming. Whether you are thinking you don't have the willpower to do it or need more motivation, these are just excuses. Also, this is the wrong approach. Understand that willpower is just like any other muscle in your body. The more you exercise it, the stronger it becomes. Initially, it might be weak, but you can improve it with practice.

So, you must first pick a habit so small that saying "no" becomes difficult. For instance, if you want to start exercising and become fit, start small instead of thinking about everything you have to do. Start with something as simple as "Today, I will exercise for five minutes." Don't you think it is easy to exercise for five minutes, and isn't it doable? When you finish the five minutes, you can perhaps challenge yourself to work for six minutes the following day. If you keep doing this daily, you will get into the groove of exercising before you know it.

Do It Daily

Consistency is crucial when it comes to making a change. If you want to develop a habit, you must do it daily. Using the information given in the previous step, you can ensure that the habit is so small that you will struggle to say "no."

Now, ensure that you do it daily. Even if it is just a 1% improvement per day, go ahead and do it. Within no time, you will see progress. This progress will give you the motivation to keep going.

Break It Into Chunks

If you follow the steps mentioned above, you will soon see progress. However, it is important to sustain this level of progress. If not, it will reduce your motivation to keep going. Therefore, the next step is to break a big habit into chunks. For instance, if you want to exercise for an hour daily, why don't you break it down into two chunks of 30 minutes each? By doing this, tackling the task becomes easier. The idea is to not just build momentum but maintain it, too.

It Is Okay to Slip

One of the most important aspects of building a new habit is to forgive yourself if you fail to stick to it. If you want to improve your self-control, then you must know how and why you lost it in the first place. Everyone makes mistakes. Even the most successful individuals have failed and made mistakes at some point or another. The only difference is that they quickly got back on track instead of giving up.

Even if you miss your habit once, it is okay. In fact, missing at once or twice doesn't stall your long-term progress. What gets in the way is an all-or-nothing attitude. Thinking that unless you do it all you have failed is problematic. For instance, if you cannot exercise for an hour on a given day, do it for as long as possible. The result of this will be better than not doing anything. You don't have to be perfect all the time. Instead, aim for consistency. Instead of expecting failure, simply plan to deal with it.

Apart from all this, simply be patient. Remember the

story of the hare and tortoise? Slow and steady wins the race! You don't have to transform yourself overnight. Not only is this impossible, but it also sets you up for failure. Instead, the progress should be such that you don't burn yourself out because burnout can quickly stall your progress.

So, simply get started and keep going. Breaking bad habits, developing new ones, and managing stress are all related. All habits offer some benefits. Most of the benefits you think you obtain from unhelpful habits are psychological. This is because the most powerful tool at your disposal is your mind. Learning to regulate it will help you achieve all the goals you desire. Read on to discover how you can do this!

If you are enjoying this book, please take a few minutes to scan the below QR code to place an Amazon review. Thank you.

IT STARTS IN THE MIND

*W*ords are incredibly powerful. The power of words is something you cannot overlook. They can be a source of your stress or worsen what you are already experiencing. Words also have the power to hurt and heal. The problem with words is that once uttered, they cannot be taken back. However, it isn't just the words uttered to others that you must be mindful of; you must be mindful of how you talk to yourself. We usually have an internal conversation going on with ourselves. This is known as self-talk.

Negative words can activate those parts of the brain that are usually active when dealing with a threat. Since the brain cannot distinguish between real and perceived danger, the stress response is triggered. When you speak negative words constantly, it shifts your brain into stress mode. This further increases the chances of negative thinking. You don't have to get stressed or worried reading all this. You have power over what you say. You can consciously decide what, how, and when you say it. It is time to understand how your self-talk can help tackle or worsen stress.

WHAT'S YOUR NARRATIVE?

We all have an internal voice or narrator that narrates the happenings in our lives. It also helps us create sentences before we utter them. This internal voice stems from the stories we tell ourselves about why the world and our life are the way they are. It essentially influences our thoughts, perspectives, and realities.

We acquire these stories not only from our personal experiences but also from childhood and societal conditioning. This inner narrative is often called our inner voice or inner speech. For instance, if you forget to pay your bill and are charged a fine, the inner voice might say, "Oh, I'm not any good with money," or if a relationship ends, it might say, "I'm not lovable." Understanding your inner narrative is important because it influences and shapes not just your self-image but your perception of life, too. If all this is shrouded by negativity, it becomes difficult to feel good about yourself. This, in turn, is also known to worsen the stress you are already experiencing.

Paying attention to your inner narrative is needed because it can unknowingly compound your stress. Negative thoughts, especially while dealing with challenging circumstances, can make you feel worse than you already do. They can also prevent you from taking risks or learning something new and increase the chances of getting stuck in the past. If you are overwhelmed by negativity, working on tackling stress becomes harder. The good news is that this internal narrative of yours can be changed for the better. You will learn how to do this in the following sections.

AFFIRMATIONS

Whether it is negative self-talk or limiting beliefs, engaging in them does not do you any favors. Instead, these behaviors simply worsen the stress you are already experiencing. Another problem with limiting thoughts is they turn into self-fulfilling prophecies when left unregulated. Regardless of everything you cannot control, your thoughts are always in your control. If the reality they manifest isn't something you are happy with, it is time to change things. By shifting your thoughts toward positivity, you will feel better. The simplest means to do this is by using positive affirmations.

Statements that help challenge and overcome negative thoughts might look like wishful thinking, but they are not. Instead, affirmations are about reframing your self-talk and thoughts in general. What happens when you exercise regularly? You become stronger and fitter and will feel better. Similarly, any thought that you think repeatedly becomes incredibly powerful. If these thoughts are positive, you welcome more positivity into your life. Think of using positive affirmations as an exercise in positive thinking for your mental muscles. They help reprogram your subconscious; over a period of time, they change how you think, feel, and act. Positive affirmations can be used in any aspect of your life, from tackling stress and overcoming self-criticism to improving self-esteem and breaking bad habits. The benefits associated with them are numerous.

Another wonderful thing about positive affirmations is they don't take much time to practice, and you can create them however you see fit. Using positive affirmations also makes you more aware of your self-talk. This, in turn, makes it easier to change or regulate them. When you start focusing on all things good, you will also start moving in the right direction. Combining these factors makes it easier to deal with the stress you are experiencing.

Here are a few positive affirmations you can use to challenge negative thoughts and increase positivity in your life.

- I will not give up.
- I am a work in progress.
- I believe in myself.
- I am surrounded by peace and abundance.
- I love and respect myself.

If you want to start using positive affirmations, the best time is first thing in the morning. As soon as you wake up, take a few deep breaths and think positively about yourself and the day ahead. You can use the positive affirmations mentioned above or make new ones that meet your requirements. Say them aloud clearly and loudly. Repeat the positive affirmations for a few minutes and repeat them whenever you feel a little stressed. When finished, breathe slowly and deeply for another minute or two and start your day.

MANTRAS

Just like positive affirmations, you can also use mantras to reduce your fear, tackle stress, and make yourself feel better. Mantras are nothing but a form of meditation that uses a word, sound, or phrase. The oldest known mantras are found in ancient religious texts from India, known as Vedas.

Depending on your comfort, you can either recite the mantra silently or out loud. Chanting mantras regulates stress, improves mood, increases self-awareness, promotes relaxation, and makes you more focused. Also, it hardly takes a couple of minutes to practice mantra meditation.

Mantras are known to reduce stress because they use the power of repetition along with a combination of sound, rhythm, and breath. Instead of getting overwhelmed by thoughts, mantras enable you to focus only on one thought at a time. This helps you to calm the mind and become more aware of yourself. This, in turn, makes it easier to notice whether your thoughts are helpful or not. Another reason mantras work is that they help synchronize your breathing with a specific sound or rhythm. Repeating the same phrase, word, or sentence in the same rhythm promotes calming vibrations. It is a form of meditation. So, using mantras is a great way to tackle stress.

Just like positive affirmations, mantras can be used at any time to regulate stress and make yourself feel better. Whether it is first thing in the morning or during the day, do it anytime you feel overwhelmed. Some common mantras you can use to reduce stress are given here.

- I am a leader.
- I can control my thoughts.
- I will get through my day one task at a time."
- Progress is a process.
- I trust myself.

If you want to, you can also use the sound "Om" for meditation. Simply chant "Om" as you breathe in and out slowly with your eyes closed. Do this for a couple of minutes.

While chanting mantras, silently or out loud, focus only on the sound the word or words make and nothing else. Even if you get distracted, gently guide your attention back to the mantra you are chanting.

STEP 6: MIND YOUR THOUGHTS

The sixth step to tackling stress is to regulate your thoughts. This starts with becoming aware of your thoughts. In any given situation, we are constantly thinking about various things. That said, not all of these thoughts are helpful. If your thoughts are predominantly pessimistic, it increases your stress. The good news is that your thoughts are always in your control. Instead of letting them overwhelm you, you can learn to regulate and change them. So, how do you become aware of your current thinking patterns? With a little self-introspection, you will know the answer. Here are some questions you can use along the way.

- What is one good thing you have thought about yourself today?
- When did you last criticize yourself?
- If a loved one came to you in their time of need, what would you tell them? Will it be the same thing you would tell yourself?
- What first thought pops into your head when facing a challenge or an obstacle?

If you answer these questions, you will know whether your thoughts are predominantly negative or positive. If it is the former, then there is no time like the present to change. Here are a couple of suggestions you can use to do this.

- Since your thoughts are responsible for the feelings that ultimately define your behaviors, changing them is needed. The simplest way to do this is by identifying any distortions. Grab your journal and make a note of common thoughts that pop up whenever you are dealing with a stressful situation.
- Once you have made a note of your thoughts, challenge your thinking. It doesn't automatically become the undeniable truth just because you think a certain thing. For instance, if you constantly think that you are a failure or that you are not good enough, ask yourself if this is true. Look for evidence that challenges your thoughts.
- The next step is to practice a little self-compassion. We are quite hard on ourselves. Engaging in harsh or negative self-talk is not helpful by any means. Once you are aware of the thought distortion that exists, it's time to show yourself a little compassion. To do this, imagine what your advice would be to a loved one had they come to you in the same situation you are in. Would you be harsh and critical? If not, then why are you doing this to yourself? Extend the same compassion you would give to others toward yourself.
- Now, the final step to challenge your thoughts is to identify the potential outcome of a specific thought. For instance, if you constantly think, I am not good enough or I will never succeed, how does this make you feel? On the other hand, how do you feel when you think, I can deal with this, or I am capable of facing the challenges that come along

my way? The former might weigh you down and make you feel worse. However, the latter can give you the strength needed to change the situation. So, ask yourself what you gain by holding on to negative thoughts. If there's nothing to gain, then why think about it? By consciously challenging your thoughts and weighing their pros and cons, it becomes easier to let the negativity go. Once you do this, don't forget to replace the negative or unhelpful thought with something better. You can use affirmations to do this.

You can learn to regulate your thoughts by implementing the suggestions given in this chapter. With conscious effort and practice, this is a perfectly achievable goal. When stressed, it might feel as if you are constantly bombarded by stressors from everywhere. In such situations, simply slowing down helps take stock of things. This, in turn, makes it easier to regulate stress. Read on to discover more about the art of slowing down.

THE ART OF SLOWING DOWN

*W*e are social creatures and have an innate desire for companionship. There is strength in numbers. Being socially connected can reduce stress, improve your self-worth, provide joy and comfort, prevent loneliness, and tackle anxiety. Almost everyone is on one social media platform or another. We use it to stay connected with others across the globe. However, too much of a good thing can be bad.

We live in a world where we are constantly connected. We are always plugged in, whether through instant messaging, posting photos on social media platforms, or scrolling through shared content. Unfortunately, because of this, our stress levels are also increasing. The use of social media has become a source of unhealthy comparisons, poor self-esteem, loneliness, isolation, and the extreme fear of missing out. Most believe that unless we give minute-by-minute updates on what we are doing, we are not living. We also spend a lot of time mindlessly scrolling through social media. Unfortunately, what was once good has become detrimental to our overall well-being.

We also live in an extremely busy and hectic world. We are constantly chasing one goal after another. We are completing tasks on a seemingly endless to-do list. There is no end to it. By doing this to ourselves, we forget about the gift of the moment we have. We are either worried about the future's uncertainties or constantly ruminating about a past that cannot be changed. Regardless of the past or the future, we forget what we can control by focusing on things beyond our control. The present is in your hands, and you cannot enjoy it unless you learn to slow down. This, coupled with overwhelming social media usage, adds more stress to our lives.

MEDITATION

The concept of meditation is not new. This age-old practice has become an incredibly popular way to reduce stress. Chances are that you think of monks who spend hours together sitting in silence with their eyes closed when you think of meditation. Well, this is not the only form of meditation. An important distinction you need to understand is that meditation is not related to any religion. It can be a spiritual process if you want it to be. The choice is entirely yours.

So, what is meditation? It's essentially the practice of different techniques that help focus your attention and improve your awareness. It is known to cause positive changes in your consciousness and offers a variety of benefits. Usually, while meditating, you will need to sit comfortably, clear your mind, or focus on a specific thought while getting rid of all others. Whether it is a word, sound, or phrase, you can concentrate on anything you want to. You can meditate for as long as 5 to 20 minutes or any other length of time you choose. The flexibility offered by meditation is one of the reasons why it can be easily incorporated into your daily life.

MEDITATION AND STRESS

A primary benefit of meditation is its ability to tackle stress. Staying in a prolonged state of the fight-or-flight response is detrimental to your overall well-being, including your physical and mental health. Meditation does the exact opposite of what that response does. It shifts your body into a state of relaxation. It restores a sense of calm, prevents the damaging effects of stress, and enables your body to start healing itself. How does it do this? Primarily it does this by calming your mind.

By now, you are aware of the body-mind connection. When it feels like your thoughts are racing at 100 mph, it becomes difficult to control them. It is not only overwhelming, it is also confusing. Physical relaxation is directly involved in meditation as well, giving you a double dose of relaxation that makes it easier to tackle stress. In the long term, it is also known to improve your resilience, because by changing how you view a stressful situation, you can act more positively. This makes it easier to get through the challenges of life. And, since meditation makes you more aware of your thoughts and teaches you to regulate them, it improves your mood. Instead of thinking of every challenge or hurdle as a failure, it lets you see the reality of them, and instead of getting bogged down by your thoughts, you learn to regulate and make sense of them. In this way, it makes you more resilient to stress.

As I've already mentioned, meditation makes you more mindful and aware of your thoughts. This, in turn, makes it easier to notice any negative thinking patterns. Unless you are aware of these thinking patterns, you cannot change them for the better. Besides this, meditation helps normalize your blood pressure, slow down your heart rate and breathing, improve immune functioning, and reduce the production of cortisol. It also improves creativity, reduces mental clutter, and improves focus, and is a great way to reconnect with your inner self.

SOME CONSIDERATIONS

Before you try meditation, here are some things you must always remember.

Consistency

The importance of consistency cannot be stressed enough when it comes to developing and maintaining healthy habits. To obtain all the benefits of meditation, you must do it regularly. Even if you are just meditating for five minutes daily, do it. The chances of sticking with meditation regularly increase if you are practicing short daily sessions. Once you can see the benefits for yourself, the motivation to keep doing it increases.

Practice

There is no such thing as perfection. If you keep chasing perfection, you will simply increase the stress you are experiencing. Similarly, when it comes to meditation, understand it's not about perfecting your practice. Instead, it's about simply practicing and obtaining the benefits it offers. It doesn't matter how long you meditate, your position when you do it, or how you do it. Instead, simply begin, and everything will fall into place. Remember that there is no wrong way to meditate, and as long as you can calm your mind and feel more relaxed, whatever you're doing is working.

Wandering Thoughts

We all think multiple thoughts at any given point. While meditating, some say that you are not supposed to let your mind wander. However, wandering thoughts are fine. Don't fall into the trap of believing you must do it right. Understand that learning to regulate your thoughts is a skill you will develop with practice and patience. Initially, your mind might wander every couple of seconds. However, this is not a bad thing. What you need to do is learn to let your thoughts go. Let them come and go. Do not fix them or try to change them. Instead, simply learn to stay in the moment. This is the real point of meditation.

TIPS TO GET STARTED

While meditating, here are a couple of tips that will help improve the overall experience and further calm your mind.

One of meditation's most important elements is learning to focus your attention. Unless you do this, you cannot free your mind of unnecessary distractions that are the source of stress or worry. Find a focal point when concentrating on a mantra, word, image, object, or your breathing. Whenever your mind gets distracted, simply return to the focal point, and it becomes easier to calm yourself.

Pay attention to your breathing while meditating. You need to breathe in and out slowly and deeply. Ensure your breathing is even. Avoid taking shallow breaths or breathing rapidly. This simply increases stress. Instead, breathe in slowly through your nose and breathe out through your mouth. You can also refocus your attention on your breathing and regain control whenever you get distracted.

Ensure you find a quiet (or at least a distraction-free) place to meditate. If too much is happening in the external environment, you cannot calm your mind or body. While meditating, even for five minutes, keep all distractions away. Put your phone on silent, turn it off if you want to, and play some relaxing music in the background. Once you get into the groove of meditation, you can learn to practice it even in noisy or distracting environments. Until then, try to create a distraction-free setting.

While meditating, different thoughts will come and go. View them from the perspective of a neutral spectator. Do not judge or criticize your thoughts. Do not try to read into them. Do not think much about them. Instead, let them come and go.

Ensure you are comfortable before you start meditating. Whether sitting, lying down, standing, or walking, ensure you are comfortable. When you are physically comfortable, it becomes easier to calm your mind.

Journaling

Journaling is the simple practice of maintaining a journal or a diary to explore your thoughts, feelings, ideas, and emotions surrounding different life events. Journaling is a wonderful way to reduce the stress you are experiencing, along with self-exploration and awareness. The simplest way to regulate the stress you are experiencing is by simply noting all that you are thinking and feeling at a given point. So, how does journaling tackle stress?

This activity helps clarify your thoughts and feelings.

This, in turn, improves your self-awareness and understanding. At times, thoughts can be quite confusing in our heads. Putting them down in words makes it easier to make sense of them. This helps to problem-solve, too.

Similarly, when it feels as if your thoughts are racing at 100 mph, making sense of them becomes challenging. If you feel overwhelmed, it becomes tough to think clearly and logically. This can further worsen the stress you are already under. As powerful as the human mind is, at times, it spends a lot of time catastrophizing, especially in situations where you are facing a challenge or an obstacle. Understand that it is almost always worse in your head than it actually is. So, a simple way to manage this is through journaling.

Apart from counteracting the effects of stress, journaling can also improve your cognitive functioning, increase your sense of gratitude, and aid positive thinking.

TRY THESE TECHNIQUES

There are different types of techniques you can use while journaling. Here are some ideas you can try.

Emotion Release

Writing about your emotional responses to events that made you feel stressed is also a type of journaling. You simply need to start writing your version of the events along with how you felt before, during, and after the said event. Doing this will give you a better sense of what triggered your emotions and stress. You can use this to reframe your opinions and explore your feelings. You can also use this to document any positive experiences you had. By doing this, you can savor the positive feelings. Think of this technique as an emotional dump. Write whatever you are feeling or thinking about it. Once you put it all out on paper, you can make more sense of it. Chances are you might stumble across unhealthy emotional responses to stress, too.

Gratitude Journal

A gratitude journal is exactly what it sounds like. In this, you are supposed to note things you are grateful for. It can also be used to make a note of all your day's highlights or things that made you feel better and positive. This is an incredible strategy to relieve stress because it shifts your focus toward everything you already have in life and everything that makes you feel better. In the long run, it creates a more positive mindset and builds resilience. Another benefit is you will be left with a detailed record of all the nice things that have happened to you throughout the day. So whenever you feel a little low in the future, you simply need to flip through the pages and you will feel better.

Bullet Journal

You can also use journals to make a note of all you want to achieve every day, from the memories you want to create, the things you don't want to forget, or even the goals you want to achieve. When you write things down, it becomes easier to remember them. It also helps you unclutter your mind and remember all that's important. This, in turn, can reduce your stress. Being unorganized definitely makes you more stressed. So this type of journaling adds a little sense of organization and balance to your life.

While journaling, ensure you don't judge or criticize yourself for your writing. Instead, simply let the words pour out. If something warrants thinking, you can introspect later. It is okay even if the sentences don't make sense, and don't look for grammatical correctness. The idea is to lighten your heart and mind. Also, consider doing this in the evening or right before bed to quickly review your day and plan for the following one. If you really want to obtain the stress-reducing benefits of journaling, you need to do it regularly and not just once.

Practicing Gratitude

Gratitude is incredibly powerful. Most of us are good at focusing on all things missing or absent in our lives. Unfortunately, we forget about the good we already have. Even though we readily have access to gratitude, we forget about that most of the time. Cultivating gratitude is extremely simple and hardly takes any time. Once you start practicing it, it'll make you feel better physically and mentally. When you focus on all the good in your life, you will feel better. This helps tackle any stress you are experiencing. It also improves your existing relationships and assists in building new ones. Whether it is thanking someone who helped you or even something as simple as opening the door for someone else, go ahead and do it. You will feel better about yourself by sending a few positive vibes to another person.

It also strengthens your relationships. You will feel better when you can see how much others do for you. This will make you more empathetic. Combining these factors will improve your self-esteem, tackle stress, and work wonders for your overall mental and emotional health.

So, how can you practice gratitude? Here are some simple suggestions that can be incorporated into your daily life to live with gratitude.

- As mentioned in the previous point, you can try gratitude journaling. Make a note of at least three things you are grateful for each day.

- Are there people in your life that you love or appreciate? Why don't you take the time to tell them so? Learn to value all the relationships in your life.
- Pause for a moment and appreciate the beauty of everything around you. Nature is incredible, and it provides everything you need. Send a heartfelt thank you to Mother Nature.
- Watch, read, or listen to something inspiring or motivating. It will remind you that there is plenty of good in the world for which you can be grateful.
- Engage in one act of kindness every day. It doesn't have to be anything major. Even something as simple as complimenting someone is sufficient.
- If there is a charitable cause close to your heart, contribute to it. Volunteer in a charitable organization and do your bit for it.
- Consciously add at least one new item to your gratitude list every day.
- Try not to complain for a week; instead, look at all things you are blessed with.
- Spend more time with those who make you feel better about yourself. Keep in touch with them. Is there a friend, family member, or someone else you have been meaning to talk to but haven't done it yet? Simply pick up the phone and call them!

STEP 7: SLOW DOWN AND APPRECIATE THE LITTLE THINGS

You need to slow down to really appreciate the little things in life. As mentioned, meditation is an excellent means of doing this. Try this simple guided meditation to slow down and calm your mind.

Find a quiet spot for yourself. Get rid of all distractions. And make yourself comfortable. Once all this is done, the next step is to close your eyes. Slowly shift all your attention to your breathing. Breathe slowly and deeply through your nose. Breathe in, fill your lungs with air. Breathe out and empty them. As you inhale, visualize a calming white light entering your body. As you breathe out, visualize all the negative thoughts you have accumulated leaving your body. Keep breathing in and out while doing this. Now start visualizing a snow globe. This snow globe is a representation of your mind. Breathe in slowly and deeply. Now, shake this mental snow globe as hard as you possibly can and start counting backward from 10.

Ten, nine, eight, seven, six, five, four, three, two, and one.

At one, stop shaking the snow globe and watch it settle. The snow that's settling is your thoughts. As the imaginary snow is settling, feel your thoughts also gradually settle. Breathe out the stress you are experiencing. Visualize that just like the globe, all of your thoughts have come to a halt. Your mind is calm. You are radiating calmness and are being engulfed by it. As you look at your mental snow globe, take a deep breath in and breathe in the peace and calm. Your mind is now quiet. With your eyes closed, slowly count to 10.

One, two, three, four, five, six, seven, eight, nine, and ten.

Open your eyes. Hold on to the peace and calm you experienced. Now, it is time to move on to the next step.

Once you feel calmer, let's practice a little gratitude. Use the questions given here to get started.

- What is one thing you are thankful for today?

- What is one personality trait of yours that makes you happy?
- What are three things that you love about your day?

Here are a few additional tips you can use to appreciate the little things in life.

Wake up 15 minutes earlier than you normally do. It might make you groan but do it anyway. You might feel a little dizzy initially, but this gives you a chance to notice all of the sensations you usually don't. This is especially true if you usually have rushed mornings. Maybe step outside for a couple of minutes to take everything in. Simply stand still and notice everything that's happening around you. Don't focus on the negatives; instead, think of a few good things around you.

Why don't you go for a long walk? Even if it is just for 15–20 minutes, do it. A simple change in scenery is known to reduce stress. It's even better if you can go for a walk in a park or any other natural space such as a wildlife preserve. If not, simply walk around the block and notice everything you see. Take in your surroundings; be present while walking, and focus on everything you see. It will become even more interesting if a loved one accompanies you.

Most of us prefer texting as the normal means of communication. Instead, why don't you try the old-fashioned approach of meeting someone face-to-face? If that's not possible for any reason, call them up and talk to them. Set aside around 15 minutes per day to talk to your loved ones. Sharing stories, exchanging gossip, or engaging in deep conversations will make you feel better. It also improves the quality of your relationships.

Another simple way to enjoy the little things in life is by focusing on an activity that you love. Whether it is reading, dancing, playing a sport, or anything else, engage in it. It will improve your overall satisfaction quotient, make you happier, and reduce your stress.

Another simple way to slow down and appreciate the little things in life is to eat slowly. Savor your meal instead of gulping it down. Avoid eating mindlessly in front of the TV or while watching something. Perhaps you can share a meal with a loved one! Enjoy all the different textures and smells of what you are eating. Be grateful for the food on your plate. Enjoy it.

YOU SNOOZE, YOU WIN

*A*re you tired of late nights and tiring days? Do you feel you have no energy when you wake up? Or perhaps you struggle to fall asleep. Waking up in the morning might feel like a battle that you keep losing with the alarm clock. Every day you tell yourself that you will go to sleep early and wake up early. However, as the night falls, you are wide awake, and the clock keeps ticking away. This fills you with stress that you cannot fall asleep and will feel tired in the morning. And the cycle goes on and on. Ultimately, you are left feeling exhausted. All this is because you aren't getting the sleep your body and mind need. You cannot function optimally if you are running on fumes. Sleep is not only restorative but is healing, too. It helps your body and mind calm down and recuperate as they prepare for the following day.

A couple of sleepless nights are fine. However, if this is the norm, then you are heading toward trouble. Sleep deprivation is detrimental to your overall well-being. It is also a source of chronic stress. Another unfortunate fact about sleep deprivation is it is also a symptom of chronic stress. So, lack of proper sleep not only makes you more stressed, but the added stress prevents you from sleeping. Phew, this is a vicious cycle; the sooner you learn to break free of it, the better. Have you ever encountered the phrase, "You snooze, you lose?" Well, it turns out this is wrong. You lose when you don't get sufficient sleep at night. In this chapter, let's discover the connection between sleep and stress and some simple tips to improve your sleep quality.

THE SCIENCE BEHIND SLEEP

The period of rest alternating with being awake is known as sleep. Your body has an internal clock responsible for regulating when you are awake and when it is time to sleep. These clocks usually have a cycle of 24 hours that are synchronized with the regular day-night cycle. Various factors regulate the internal clock, ranging from light and darkness to sleep schedules. Once you are asleep, you go through different stages of sleep throughout the night in a predictable pattern. Sleep is one of the most important aspects of maintaining your overall health. Not getting sufficient sleep is detrimental to not just your physical health, but also to your mental health.

UNDERSTANDING SLEEP-WAKE CYCLES

Did you know that your body has an internal clock? This clock is responsible for regulating your sleep-wake cycles. Your internal clock is known as a circadian clock. Circadian clocks usually follow the 24-hour repeating rhythm known as the circadian rhythm. This affects all cells, organs, and tissues in your body and influences how they work. The central circadian clock is housed in the brain. It essentially tells the brain when it is time to sleep. Other circadian clocks are present in different organs throughout your body. These clocks are in sync with your body's external cues from your surroundings. Light and darkness are common cues determining when you feel awake and when you feel tired.

Most of us have a circadian cycle that's longer than 24 hours. This is one of the reasons why some people can wake up quite early in the morning while others stay up late at night. For instance, teenagers usually prefer later bedtimes and wake later in the morning when compared to adults. The natural rhythm, along with the timing of the internal body clock, reduce with age. Neurons or brain cells that are responsible for promoting sleep are usually lost during the normal aging process. This usually makes it harder for older adults to stay asleep for long. Other lifestyle factors, such as less time spent outdoors or leading a sedentary lifestyle, also affect natural circadian rhythms. This is one of the reasons why your ability to fall asleep later at night and wake up later in the morning reduces with age.

The human body is quite intuitive and has a biological need for sleep. This need increases as the time you are awake increases. The cycle is regulated by a process known as hemostasis, which is responsible for keeping all of your internal systems in balance. This is the same process that regulates your internal body temperature. A compound known as adenosine is also associated with this inherent need for sleep. When awake, the levels of adenosine in the brain increase gradually. These rising levels signal your brain that it needs to sleep. Certain stimulants such as caffeine, nicotine, alcohol, and even some drugs interrupt this process and block adenosine production. This, in turn, disrupts your sleep-wake cycle.

Apart from this, the light-dark cycle also plays a role in your ability to sleep. If you are following the natural day and night schedule, the light signals your eyes receive tell the brain it is daytime. Upon receiving this signal, a specific part of the brain signals your body to stay awake when there is daylight. This essentially means that your body's central clock is in sync with the natural day-night cycle. Exposure to artificial lights, such as those emitted by electronic gadgets and devices, interferes with this process.

How does this happen? The light-dark cycle influences the brain to produce a hormone known as melatonin. Melatonin travels to different cells in your body through the bloodstream. As evening approaches, melatonin production increases. This production peaks early in the morning. Melatonin is known to promote your ability to sleep through the night. As your body is gradually exposed to more light, such as the rising sun's rays, another hormone, cortisol, is released. Cortisol prepares your body to wake up in the morning. Prolonged exposure to artificial light disturbs this process and confuses your body. If you are used to spending some time on your phone scrolling through social media or watching television before bedtime, your mind is tricked into believing that it is not yet night. This, in turn, disrupts melatonin production and increases cortisol production. This ultimately means you will struggle to fall asleep at night.

SLEEP PHASES AND STAGES

Whenever you sleep, you go through two phases of sleep cyclically. The first phase is known as rapid eye movement (REM) sleep, and the second is known as non-REM sleep. After every 80–100 minutes, the cycle starts all over again. Usually, we go through 4–6 cycles every night. In between these cycles, you might be awake for brief periods.

During the first stage, which is REM sleep, your eyes start twitching, and the brain is still active. Brain activity during this stage of sleep is almost the same as its activity when awake. Dreaming usually occurs in this stage of sleep. Your muscles, however, become limp, which ensures you are not acting out your dreams in real life. If the temperature is too cold, you do not have as much REM sleep as you normally would. This is because the body temperature isn't well-regulated during this stage.

Non-REM sleep has three stages, and your brain activity measures each. During the first stage, the brain shifts from wakefulness to the stage of sleep. In the second stage, you are asleep. The third stage is known as slow-wave sleep or deep sleep. Usually, we spend most of our time in this stage early in the night after going to bed.

THE IMPORTANCE OF SLEEP

You cannot be healthy if you cannot get sufficient sleep. It plays a vital role in how you feel when awake and with your energy levels. While asleep, your body kickstarts various internal processes that support cognitive functioning and the maintenance of your physical health. Inadequate sleep increases the risk of chronic health problems in the long run.

It also influences how you think, react, learn, work, and even get along with those around you. In this section, let's see how sleep affects different aspects of your health.

When you enter the non-REM stage of sleep, your heart rate and blood pressure reduce. The parasympathetic system regulates your body, and the heart doesn't have to work as hard as it normally does when awake. The sympathetic system is activated during the REM stage of sleep and when waking. This increases your heart rate and blood pressure levels to the levels they usually are when you are relaxed or awake. Those who do not get the required sleep are at an increased risk of developing various health problems, such as obesity, strokes, cardiovascular disorders, and hypertension.

A variety of hormones are produced in your body at different times of the day. Hormones are chemical messengers that essentially control all bodily processes and functions. The rate at which certain hormones are produced is associated with your sleep patterns or circadian rhythm. Usually, hormones that promote alertness are released in the morning, which helps you wake up. At night, your body produces other hormones that make it easier to fall asleep. If inadequate sleep has become the norm, it disrupts the hormonal balance. Hormonal imbalance is associated with various health conditions related to different systems in your body.

Sleep also plays an important role in how your body handles fats. Depending on the circadian rhythm, your body decides whether it needs to use or store fat in the liver and muscles. For instance, during the day, your body ensures the liver is prepared to digest fats at certain times. If you eat at unusual times, your body's ability to deal with the fat stored within also differs. If you don't get sufficient sleep, it directly affects your metabolism. It can result in higher levels of hunger due to excess production of leptin and ghrelin. Similarly, it can also increase the risk of insulin resistance and metabolic syndromes such as type-2 diabetes. Combining all these factors can ultimately result in obesity when left unregulated.

Sleep deprivation affects your cognitive functioning, thinking, and memory. Usually, when you sleep at night, the brain gets a chance to process all the information absorbed during the day and store it as memories. If you are not getting adequate rest, it will affect your memory. Apart from it, you might notice that focusing on simple tasks becomes difficult, and your ability to think clearly also takes a backseat when sleep deprived.

HOW MUCH SLEEP IS SUFFICIENT?

So, how much sleep do you really need? Did you know that adults require around seven to nine hours of undisturbed sleep at night? Yes, this is true. Even if you can survive on five hours of sleep per night, it is not healthy in the long run. Sleeping for less than seven hours results in a variety of health problems. When it comes to sleep, it's not just the duration but the quality of sleep that matters too. For instance, don't think that catching up on naps during the day will help make up for the sleep you don't get at night. Even if naps and nighttime sleep together account for seven hours, it is not helpful. In fact, napping during the day prevents you from sleeping properly at night. What you need is sound sleep for seven hours straight. This means once you are asleep, you shouldn't wake up until the alarm wakes you up in the morning. Even if you wake up, you should be able to fall asleep again. If you struggle to fall asleep, find yourself awake at odd times, and struggle to wake up in the morning, these are all signs of insufficient sleep.

STRESS VS. SLEEP

Around 35% of adults in the US reportedly sleep for less than seven hours per night, according to the 2017 findings of the Centers for Disease Control and Prevention. This is a worrying number. As mentioned, adults need around seven hours of undisturbed sleep per night. The ramifications of improper, poor, or inadequate sleep are serious. Being used to inadequate sleep almost daily results in various mental and physical health problems.

If you don't sleep sufficiently at night, it reduces your energy levels the following day. It can put you in a negative mood and disrupt your usual ability to function. It also makes it difficult to concentrate or stay focused on specific tasks. In some circumstances, lack of sleep or sleep deprivation has severe consequences, especially if you are engaged in activities such as driving or operating heavy machinery. It is perfectly fine if poor sleep is only a rare or occasional occurrence. However, being mostly sleep-deprived increases the risk of different chronic health conditions, including obesity, depression, heart diseases, diabetes, arthritis, kidney problems, and strokes.

By now, you know all the negative connotations associated with chronic stress. The fight or flight response that helped humans in their early survival has now become a problem. One of the most harmful effects of stress on your body is sleep deprivation. If you are in a heightened state of alertness for prolonged periods, it delays the onset of sleep and causes rapid and anxious thoughts at night. This, in turn, makes it difficult to fall and stay asleep.

Insufficient sleep is also known to further worsen the effect of stress you are already experiencing. This is one of the reasons why thinking about different thoughts makes it difficult to fall asleep at night. If you don't get sufficient rest at night, you will feel low on energy, experience a poor mood, and will feel tired most of the time. This, in turn, can further worsen the stress you are already under. The only way to end this vicious cycle is by learning to manage your stress. You can also change your sleep schedule to ensure your body and mind get the rest they deserve and need.

WAYS TO IMPROVE SLEEP QUALITY

Perhaps your sleep schedule is no longer working for you. Maybe you are staying up later than intended or are struggling to wake up in the morning. Or perhaps even when you sleep, you don't feel refreshed or well-rested in the morning. So, what can be done in such a situation? As with any other aspect of your lifestyle and health, even your sleep is in your control. By resetting your sleep schedule, you can improve the overall quality of your sleep. In this section, let's look at some simple suggestions that will come in handy.

If you want to improve the quality of your sleep at night, the first thing you need to do is create a sleep schedule. This means you need to adjust your bedtime such that it works well for your usual lifestyle. Usually, it's quite easy for us to stay up for an hour longer than to go to sleep an hour earlier. However, you can slowly retrain your body and mind to fall asleep and wake up at a specific time. Don't opt for a schedule that is not realistic or practically sustainable. For instance, if you know you have to wake up early in the morning, then going to bed at midnight doesn't make any sense. Even if you can do it for a couple of days, your resilience to it will soon fizzle out. Instead, opt for a schedule that works well for you. You are good to go if you get at least seven hours of undisturbed sleep per night. Once the schedule is in place, you need to stick to it.

A common mistake most people make is that we believe we can catch up on our night's sleep by napping during the day. If you keep napping throughout the day, falling asleep at night becomes challenging. Even a 30-minute nap later in the evening can mess with your sleep schedule. To ensure this doesn't happen, avoid daytime naps as much as you can. Even if you feel incredibly tired, simply push yourself to get through the day. You can go to sleep early instead of napping.

Do you usually spend some time scrolling through social media before sleeping? Or perhaps you watch one of your favorite TV series. Whatever it is, ensure that you do not expose yourself to bright blue light right before bedtime. This is because blue light is known to interfere with your internal clock, which is responsible for regulating your sleep-wake cycle. This clock is easily tricked by different devices and screens that emit bright lights, especially blue light. This light essentially tricks your brain into believing that it is daytime. When this happens, your brain automatically becomes more awake and alert. This, in turn, results in difficulty getting to sleep.

You also need to pay attention to what you eat before bedtime. Certain foods disrupt your internal metabolism and prevent you from sleeping. It's not just stimulants that keep your mind alert. Acidic or spicy foods are known to trigger acid reflux or heartburn. Similarly, eating heavy meals right before bedtime prevents a good night's sleep. Ensure that there are at least two to three hours between your last meal and bedtime. This gives your body sufficient time to process the food you have eaten. This, in turn, makes it easier to fall asleep.

If you really want to reset your sleep schedule, you need to commit to this process. It takes time and plenty of effort to reset your sleep schedule. Once you commit to it, you can do it.

STEP 8: FOCUS ON SLEEP QUALITY

By now, you are aware of the simple fact that good quality sleep is crucial to your overall well-being. It also offers different stress-reducing benefits. However, when it comes to sleep, apart from following a good sleep routine and engaging in good sleep hygiene, you need to focus on the quality of sleep, as well. If you usually wake up in the middle of the night, struggle to go back to sleep after waking up, or don't feel well-rested in the morning, it is all due to poor quality of sleep. Here are some simple tips you can use to improve your quality of sleep.

The first thing you need to do is ensure your bedroom is a sleep-inducing environment. The room needs to be dark and cool for sound slumber. Consider different options to create an environment conducive to sleep, from heavy curtains to earplugs. The room should not only be well-ventilated, but it should be noise-free, dark, and the temperature must be comfortable. The bedroom is meant for sleeping and intimate time. Any other activity should be performed in some other room of the house.

Apart from avoiding heavy meals right before bedtime, it is important that you do not consume any stimulants later in the day. Whether it is caffeine, alcohol, or nicotine, avoid them as much as you can, especially before bedtime. These stimulants can keep you awake and alert. So, avoid them at least four to six hours before bedtime.

Create and follow a calming pre-sleep routine. This routine will help shift your mind from being awake to going to sleep. Ideally, do this right before bedtime. Whether it is taking a warm bath, reading a book, writing in your gratitude journal, or meditating, do something that relaxes your body and mind. When you are calmer, it becomes easier to fall asleep.

If you wake up in the middle of the night, avoid staring at the clock. Don't worry about the time ticking by. Instead, engage in any of your preferred pre-sleep routine activities to calm your mind and body once again.

As a rule of thumb, ensure that you stick to your sleep schedule. Once you have decided on your bedtime and when you wake up in the morning, follow it without any breaks. Stick to the sleep schedule, whether it is the weekend, a weekday, or a holiday. All it takes is one late night to derail the progress you make.

If you are exercising in the evening, ensure there is at least a three-hour gap between working out and bedtime. Exercise stimulates your body and mind. This keeps your brain active, and falling asleep becomes a struggle.

Finally, ensure that you follow the different tips and suggestions you were introduced to in this chapter to improve your sleep schedule. These steps shouldn't be taken occasionally; instead, they must become a part of your daily routine. You might not see a change immediately, but eventually, the overall quality of your sleep will improve.

Sleep, especially good quality sleep, is needed for your overall well-being. When you are well-rested, it becomes easier to manage the stress you are experiencing. It also improves your energy levels. Now that you have learned to improve your sleep quality let us move on to the next aspect of managing stress by shifting to a healthier lifestyle. This is to add some exercise to your daily routine. Are you wondering how you can do it? Move on to the next chapter to learn about this!

GO WITH THE FLOW

*W*e all know that exercise is good for the body. However, it becomes challenging when we are too busy or stressed to fit it into our routine. Woah, hold on! There is plenty of good news when it comes to exercise and its positive effects on stress. Any form of exercise, whether it is yoga or aerobics, helps relieve your stress. It doesn't matter if you are out of shape, are not athletic, or think you are too busy; you can still make a little exercise go a very long way when managing stress.

MOVE WITH INTENTION

If you regularly tell yourself that you will start exercising tomorrow and that day never seems to come, it is time to take conscious action. Exercise works wonders for your physical and mental well-being. Once you know all the benefits it offers, the inherent motivation needed to start exercising and sticking to a schedule will improve. Here are some stress-busting effects of exercise.

A major benefit of exercise is that it increases the production of feel-good neurotransmitters known as endorphins. Whether it is a hike in nature or an engaging game of tennis, it pumps you full of these helpful neuro-transmitters. These are known to improve your overall mood, counteract the effect of stress, and make you feel better.

Exercise offers the needed relief for your body while limiting the harmful effects of stress, such as the onset and maintenance of the fight or flight response. It ensures your body and all systems within are working together as a unit to tackle the effect of stress. Regular exercise improves the functioning of your cardiovascular, digestive, and immune systems. Combining these makes your body more resilient to stress and its effects.

Whether it is a long walk or a couple of laps in the pool, you will soon forget about the day's irritations after a little physical activity. This is because exercise is nothing less than meditation in motion. If you are leading a sedentary lifestyle, change things up with some physical activity. This change in pace itself is a much-needed break and distraction for your body and mind. This is one of the reasons why we feel more energetic and optimistic after engaging in any physical activ-ity. It enables you to stay calmer and logically think through any challenges you face instead of giving in to stress. Also, regular physical activity promotes better sleep at night. This, in turn, also helps tackle stress.

Another benefit of regular exercise is it helps you get fitter and stronger. If you have been struggling to shed those extra pounds, then start exercising. When your body feels good, you will feel better about yourself. In a way, it improves your self-esteem and confidence. These things, coupled with a better mood and an improved ability to relax, will make you feel better inside and out.

In the next sections, you will learn more about simple tips that can be used to incorporate exercise into your daily routine.

Note: Yes, exercise is incredibly beneficial and offers a variety of benefits. However, if you have any existing health problems, don't forget to consult your healthcare provider before starting a new physical routine. For instance, some types of exercise aren't recommended for people who suffer from joint pain. Similarly, the intensity and duration of the exercises performed matter, too. So, consult your healthcare provider, and only then should you start exercising.

NO TIME? NO PROBLEM

Tensing of the muscles, random pains and aches, digestive troubles, and rapid breathing are all physical manifestations of stress. Stress harms not only your mental health but your physical well-being, too.

By now, you are aware of the different reasons why regular exercise is good for your body and mind. Apart from all this, exercise is also an excellent means to tackle stress. Now, you might wonder how you can make exercise a part of your daily life if you don't have the time for it. Well, don't you worry because there is an option for you, too! The answer is quite simple. You can add some mental exercises to your routine. Sure, they don't offer the physical benefits of exercise, but even mental exercises tackle stress. Also, when you feel better mentally, you will feel better physically. When you are calmer and more in control of yourself, taking some time out for regular exercise becomes easier.

If you think, *But I don't have the time for this,* think again. Here are some extremely simple exercises you can perform to tackle stress.

Breathing Exercises

When stressed, your breathing becomes erratic, shallow, and rapid. On the other hand, if you are breathing slowly, deeply, and evenly, it is a sign of relaxation. By learning to control your breathing, you can mimic the overall effect of relaxation. What is the result? You will feel more relaxed and less stressed. Here is a simple deep breathing exercise you can use.

1. Close your eyes and breathe in slowly and deeply. Push your stomach out and engage the diaphragm while doing this.
2. Hold your breath for two seconds.
3. Exhale slowly through your nose and repeat the word "relax" in your mind.
4. Repeat the sequence 10 times and concentrate only on breathing slowly and deeply.
5. If you do this, you can easily normalize your breathing. This, in turn, will make you feel calmer and relaxed.

Mental Exercises

Physical exercise relaxes the mind. Similarly, mental exercises relax your mind. Usually, talking to someone about your problems helps you achieve this goal. However, you can also harness the power of your own mind and reduce the stress you are experiencing.

Previously, you were introduced to the concept of journaling. Apart from this, another classic example of uniting your body and mind is meditation. Mental stress increases your blood pressure, heart rate, and breathing. All this can be normalized by meditating. Here is a simple meditation exercise that can be used to improve your relaxation response.

1. Start by finding a quiet and private spot for yourself. Ensure that you will be left uninterrupted and without distractions for this meditation. It hardly takes around 20 minutes.

2. Choose a body position that allows your body to relax fully. The idea is to get comfortable. Now, start breathing slowly and deeply. You can use the breathing exercise you were introduced to in the previous section to do this.

3. Close your eyes and block external stimuli. This is needed to achieve a passive and relaxed mental state. This means trying to get your mind to go as blank as possible. Let go of all worries and thoughts. Even if they come, simply let them pass instead of holding on to them.

4. Now, it is time to concentrate on a mental device of your choice. Whether it is a phrase, syllable, simple word, or mantra, you simply need to repeat it chant-like. You can either repeat them silently in your mind or say them out loud. The act of repetition is incredibly powerful. Even if it is just one word, it helps calm your mind. In a way, when doing this, your mind is solely focused on the mental device you chose. Whenever your thoughts come, simply redirect your attention to the mental device. Keep breathing normally, and that's about it.

5. Open your eyes once you feel better and get back to whatever you were doing.

Progressive Muscle Relaxation

Your muscles become tight and dense when stressed. By relaxing your muscles, you can learn to let go of the stress you are experiencing. Muscle relaxation is a simple practice but takes a while longer than the previous exercises. However, if you can make this a part of your daily routine, you will feel better.

Progressive muscle relaxation takes around 15–20 minutes. You need to sequentially focus on all of the major muscle groups in your body. While doing it, you need to tighten the muscle consciously and maintain that tension for 20 seconds. After this, slowly release the muscle. As the muscle relaxes, focus on expelling any stress or tension you are experiencing. Allow the sensation of relaxation to flood all over your body. Start with your facial muscles and slowly work your way down toward your feet.

Once your breathing is normalized, focus all your attention on your facial muscles. Tighten them. You can do this by wrinkling your forehead, clenching your jaw, or arching your eyebrows. Hold this for 20 seconds, then slowly start relaxing the muscles. Visualize that stress and worry are slowly leaving your body as the muscles relax.

You will simply need to repeat the same process with all the other muscle groups in your body. Once you reach the feet and have relaxed all the muscles, you will feel calmer and less stressed.

The Flow

The popularity of yoga is steadily increasing and for all the right reasons. More and more people are becoming aware of its various physical and mental health benefits. Yoga offers different benefits, from reducing stress and improving physical fitness to self-awareness and improvement. Understand that yoga is not just restricted to physical postures but includes relaxation techniques and meditation, too. So, adding yoga to your daily routine is a wonderful idea to improve your overall sense of well-being.

Before doing this, let's see how yoga alleviates stress and anxiety. It encourages mental and physical relaxation. The physical postures prescribed by it promote flexibility, relieve muscular tension, and can alleviate pain you are experiencing. When you feel better physically, your mental health improves. The release of feel-good hormones while performing yoga further counteracts the effects of stress. Another benefit of yoga is it promotes awareness. It encourages you to consciously focus on the moment right now and nothing else. Once you become more aware of your bodily sensations, feelings, thoughts, and emotions, regulating them becomes easier. You can let go of unhelpful thoughts and replace them with healthier and more helpful ones.

The stress-relieving benefits of yoga cannot be emphasized enough. However, to achieve these benefits, you need to practice regularly. It's not something you do once and then forget about for the rest of the week. Since yoga also promotes mindfulness, you also learn to regulate your thoughts. It helps you stay in the moment instead of worrying about the future or getting stuck in the past. You can let go of all things that are holding you back and create room for some positivity.

As mentioned, yoga isn't just restricted to physical postures. Instead, it includes a variety of breathing exercises, known as pranayama in Sanskrit. These exercises teach you to relax by regulating your breath and focusing only on it. It simultaneously calms your body and mind. A wonderful thing about these breathing exercises is they can be performed at any point during your day. In fact, the breathing exercises you were introduced to in the previous section can also be a part of your yoga routine.

If you are just getting started with yoga, then here are some poses you must try to relieve stress.

- Cat-cow
- Child's Pose
- Legs-Up-the-Wall
- Corpse

TIPS TO USE

Yoga certainly helps calm your body and mind. However, to make the most of its stress-relieving benefits, here are a couple of tips you must remember.

- It's important that you release negativity while performing yoga. Negative thoughts are bound to crop up from time to time. You can create healthier mental patterns by practicing awareness, acceptance, and detachment. It doesn't mean you will not have any negative thoughts; instead, it teaches you to tolerate them and not get affected by them so much.
- As mentioned, yoga and all its practices encourage you to stay in the moment. You can better understand and accept their fleeting nature by paying attention to your thoughts as they come

and go. Whatever you are thinking right now is not permanent, and it is certainly not set in stone. It also doesn't mean your thoughts are always the undeniable truth. Once you become aware of the unhelpful thoughts, replacing them with healthier ones becomes easier. Any meditation practice you opt for will teach emotional regulation.

Yoga is just one aspect of stress management. If you really want to tackle stress and keep it away, you must also employ other techniques. You can successfully tackle stress by using all the 11 steps for stress relief you will be introduced to in this book. So, look for a holistic approach to tackling stress and don't just focus on one aspect.

STEP 9: START EXERCISING

Do you keep telling yourself that you will start exercising tomorrow? But then tomorrow never comes? Or perhaps you are struggling to exercise because you don't like it. Well, whatever the reason, there is no time like the present to start exercising regularly. Here are some tips you can use to make physical activity a part of your daily routine. These tips will ensure you stay motivated, too.

A common reason why most people give up on their exercise regimen is that they do not enjoy it. When exercise feels like a chore, chances are you will start procrastinating or avoiding it. An activity that's perceived to be unenjoyable or just boring cannot become a sustainable part of your daily routine. Instead, you need to find something you truly enjoy doing. The good news is there are a variety of options available these days, whether it is joining a fitness class, going to the gym, swimming, dancing, doing yoga, running, or even playing a sport. You simply need to find and stick to one activity you like.

If you are just getting started, avoid setting unrealistic exercise goals for yourself. Most people usually carry an all-or-nothing attitude when it comes to working out. The problem is that this mindset sets you up for failure from the beginning. Instead, try to do as much as you can. You can always increase the time spent exercising. Instead of aiming for a one-hour workout every day, try exercising for 10 minutes. Ten minutes isn't much, is it? Once you are working out for 10 minutes every day, make it 20 minutes per day the following week. Slowly increase the time spent exercising. Once you see the benefits of exercise for yourself, the internal motivation needed to do it regularly will improve. Ideally, aim for around 150 minutes of exercise per week.

As with developing any new habit, getting into the groove of exercising regularly also takes practice. Adding it to your daily schedule is the best way to ensure you don't skip working out. Once you set some time aside for it, stick to the schedule. You wouldn't miss an important doctor's appointment or meeting at work, would you? Similarly, once some time has been set aside for your exercise routine, do it. If you do it at the same time daily, you will soon get used to it.

Consider exercising with a partner. Find a workout buddy for yourself. You can both help each other stick to the exercise regimen. Also, when you exercise with someone, it becomes more enjoyable. Another benefit of exercising with a partner is it automatically increases your accountability.

Well, adding exercise to your daily routine is easy. Once you are habituated to it, you can reap all the different benefits it offers. Now that sleep and physical activity are taken care of, the next healthy lifestyle change you need to make is to eat healthily. Diet and stress are also related. In the next chapter, you will learn more about this relationship and all that can be done to start eating healthily.

YOU ARE WHAT YOU EAT

*D*o you feel like eating ice cream when your mood is low? Or perhaps digging into a bowl of mac and cheese after a tiring day feels like a warm hug. This is because we often find comfort in food. They are known as comfort foods for this reason. Food is not just fuel for your body, but it can also become a coping mechanism for stress. And this is not a good thing in the long run. From obesity and unhealthy weight gain to various other chronic health problems, using food as a coping mechanism is not good. Also, not to mention the fact that food cannot solve the stress you are under. Eating away your stress might work temporarily, but it is not a solution. So, what can be done now? You can repair your relationship with food by learning to become mindful of what and when you eat. In this section, let's look at some suggestions that can be incorporated to improve your relationship with food and help you to start eating healthily.

STRESS AND FOOD

Chances are you might have come across the phrase "stress eating" before. Stress unleashes a variety of hormones, and when these hormones are coupled with the effects of sugary and unhealthy foods, the chances of overeating increase. This is one of the reasons why weight gain is associated with chronic stress. At times, stress can shut down your appetite altogether. However, after a point, you will end up overeating or binge eating.

Your food preferences are also affected when under stress. Physical or emotional distress increases the craving for foods rich in sugar, fat, or both. High levels of cortisol caused by stress, when coupled with high insulin levels, destabilize internal balances. Sugar and fat-filled foods can reduce the severity of stress-related responses and emotions. However, this is just a short-term or temporary response. It is akin to putting a bandage on a gaping wound.

If you are constantly reaching for foods you know aren't good for your body but are eating them anyhow, it is an unhealthy stress response. This is nothing to be ashamed of. We all do it at one point or another. However, it's a good sign if you have become aware of stress eating. It shows you are aware of the problem. Once you know the problem, fixing it becomes easier.

WHAT'S YOUR RELATIONSHIP WITH FOOD?

A good relationship with food involves knowing that you can eat all the foods you want because they make you feel better physically and mentally. This means you should not make some foods off-limits. For instance, you might eat a scoop of ice cream when stressed. After this, you might feel guilty. This happens because we perceive some foods as good and others as bad. However, a good relationship with food encourages you to make healthier choices because they feel better to you. Instead of doing things because you should or must, you learn to do it because you can.

Before you learn to mend your relationship with food, it's important to understand your existing one. Understand that a good relationship with food has nothing to do with the quality of your diet or the different types of food you eat. Instead, it focuses on how and why you choose to eat certain foods.

If you feel guilty about eating, avoid, or restrict foods that you believe are bad, or have a long list of rules about what you can or cannot eat, these are all signs of a poor relationship with food. Similarly, ignoring your body's hunger cues, relying solely on calorie counters, and feeling stress or anxiety about what others think about your food choices means you have a bad relationship with food. Another bad sign is binge eating. If you are doing any of these, there is no time to rectify your relationship with food like the present.

Here are some simple tips you can use to repair your relationship with food.

- Give yourself unconditional permission to eat what you want.
- Do not deprive yourself of food or fear it.
- Eat only when you are hungry and until you are full.
- Add all types of whole foods to your diet.
- Get rid of all foods that look like they were mass-produced in factories.

- Be mindful of the food choices you make.
- Increase the consumption of fruits, vegetables, lean protein, nuts and seeds, and healthy fats.

CHOOSING THE RIGHT DIET

Whenever stressed, the production of cortisol increases in your body. A simple way to counteract this is by consuming foods that lower the production of cortisol. Even though cortisol performs several helpful functions, such as regulating blood pressure, reducing inflammation, maintaining blood sugar, and managing how your body uses nutrients, it is healthy only in short bursts. After this, it's simply increasing the stress you are experiencing. Excess cortisol results in more inflammation and increased blood pressure and does almost everything opposite of good or desirable.

As mentioned, some foods are known to relieve stress. By focusing on an anti-inflammatory diet, you can achieve this goal. It means you will need to limit the consumption of processed foods and increase the intake of whole foods. The idea is to reduce inflammation in the body to reduce cortisol levels. This, in turn, combats stress. Here are some food groups that can be added to your daily diet to improve stress response.

- Foods rich in vitamin B help metabolize cortisol. Some common examples include fortified cereal, chicken, organ meat, eggs, and beef.
- Similarly, foods rich in omega-3 fatty acids also tackle inflammation. They also improve cardiovascular and cognitive functioning. Some common sources of foods rich in omega-3 fatty

acids are fatty fish, olive oil, nuts, seeds, and avocados.

- Another category of foods that need to be added to your diet are the ones rich in magnesium. Magnesium reduces inflammation, metabolizes cortisol, and relaxes the body and mind. Some common foods you can add are avocados, broccoli, pumpkin seeds, bananas, and dark chocolate.
- Protein-rich foods help stabilize blood sugar levels, and this, in turn, regulates stress. Some common examples include turkey, tuna, chicken, almonds, lentils, salmon, shrimp, and quinoa.
- Increasing the consumption of gut-healthy foods also reduces inflammation. Some common examples of foods known to promote gut health, reduce cholesterol, and stabilize blood sugar levels are kimchi, kombucha, yogurt, kefir, and sauerkraut.

Now, let's get to the list of foods you must avoid to manage stress. Also, once you eliminate or severely restrict the consumption of the items listed below, your physical health will improve, too.

- Alcohol
- High-sugar foods
- Caffeine
- Sodas
- Deep-fried foods
- Refined starches and products made with it
- Processed and packaged foods

FINDING THE RIGHT DIET

The ketogenic diet, intermittent fasting, the Mediterranean diet, Atkins, the South Beach diet, the Sonoma diet... the list of diets out there is pretty much endless. How can you find the right diet for you when there are so many to choose from? The first thing you must understand about shifting to a healthier diet is that there is no such thing as the perfect diet. Some diets work for some, while others don't. You don't have to start a diet because it seems to work for your friend. Instead, the idea is to find a diet that works well for you. It does not matter if a specific diet is scientifically sound or how many people have tried it. It is not about what you should be doing; instead, it is about what you can do.

To find the right diet, understand that it all boils down to eating healthily. It needs to be sustainable, too. A good diet increases your intake of wholesome foods instead of processed ones. It shouldn't encourage you to eat extremely small or insufficient portions. Instead, it needs to encourage you to understand your body's satiety and hunger cues. It needs to promote mindful eating. It is about reaching a stage where you are eating because you know some foods are good for you and they make you feel better. This always works in the long run instead of forcing yourself to follow a fad diet.

So, if you are looking for the right diet for yourself, here are some considerations. Use this checklist and see for yourself whether a given diet will work for you or not.

- Does the diet match your regular eating style?
- Can it accommodate your social life?
- Does the diet cater to your existing fitness level?

- Does it include foods you enjoy, can prepare, and can afford?
- Does it encourage healthier eating habits?
- Does it leave room for small and gradual changes, or is it an overnight overhaul of your eating habits?
- Is it flexible or too rigid to follow?

So, take some time and answer the questions mentioned above. Once you do this, you can see whether a specific diet will work for you. If it doesn't work, then you can always experiment with another diet. By following the different dietary suggestions you were introduced to earlier, you can start eating your way to a healthier body and mind.

IS SNACKING GOOD?

If you really want to tackle stress, then you are already aware of some basic things that you need to take care of, such as exercising regularly and getting sufficient sleep. However, did you know that you can also snack healthily to reduce stress? Yes, this is possible. One thing you need to understand about learning to manage stress through food is that it is not an overnight occurrence. Instead, it is a long game. However, you can quickly improve your energy levels and obtain a little natural assistance while unwinding through healthy snacking. Look for foods that are rich in magnesium because it helps reduce stress. This important mineral also normalizes blood pressure, strengthens your bones, and promotes a healthier heart rhythm. Here are a couple of healthy snacks to munch on and reduce stress when in a pinch.

- Dark chocolate (at least 70% cocoa)
- Herbal tea (unsweetened)
- Whole-grain bread
- Avocados
- Warm milk
- Nuts and seeds
- Citrus fruits
- Leafy greens

An important thing you must do if you are trying to reduce stress is to avoid skipping meals. Instead, develop and maintain a regular eating schedule. Eating once every three to five hours stabilizes blood sugar levels. Cortisol production increases if your blood sugar level is low because your body perceives it as a source of stress. Keeping your blood sugar balanced will improve your ability to manage stress.

Even though some foods help reduce cortisol levels, food should not be the only way to destress. Instead, you need to prioritize other means of managing stress, as well. You need to focus on all aspects of your health, not just your diet, to improve stress management.

STEP 10: WHAT ARE YOU EATING TODAY?

By now, you are well aware of diet and nutrition's role in your overall health and well-being, especially in stress management. Quality in is always equivalent to quality out when it comes to your health. So, now is the time to make a couple of healthy changes to ensure your body and mind get the required nutrients. Once you cater to the requirements of your body and mind, they will function effectively and efficiently. Here are some simple suggestions you can use to ensure you are eating healthily.

Have you ever heard the phrase "Eat the rainbow?" It essentially means you need to consume foods of different colors daily. Different colored fruits and vegetables are often filled with a variety of nutrients your body requires. The more colorful your plate is, the healthier and better it is. Increase your general consumption of fruits and vegetables. They are rich in dietary fiber, a variety of vitamins, and essential minerals. A predominantly plant-based diet reduces inflammation, improves cardiovascular functioning, and enhances physical health. This has a positive effect on your mental well-being, too.

Instead of processed foods, try to increase your consumption of wholesome and unprocessed foods. This means avoiding white rice, white flour, and products made with them as much as you can. Instead, replace them with healthy alternatives such as whole grains, brown rice, and products made with these materials. In fact, try to avoid all foods that look like they were mass-produced in a factory.

Instead of cutting out the foods you love, look for healthy alternatives. For instance, if you love French fries, why don't you replace them with a healthier alternative, such as baked sweet potatoes? Similarly, potato chips can be replaced with baked kale chips. All that it requires is a little creativity, and you can quickly turn an unhealthy dish into a healthy one. This way, you will not feel deprived of the foods you enjoy. This repairs your relationship with food. Similarly, you don't have to cut out junk food entirely. Instead, replace it with healthier versions or alternatives.

Another simple suggestion you can use to start eating healthily is to eat only when you are hungry. Also, eat until you are full. To do this, you need to practice a little mindfulness. Usually, most of us eat in a rush or eat mindlessly. We seldom pay attention to what we are eating or how much we are eating. Instead, stay present in the moment while eating. Avoid all distractions and focus only on the food you are eating. Notice its textures and different flavors. Savor every bite and eat slowly. Chew thoroughly before swallowing, and don't be in a rush. Once you do this, you will become more aware of your body's hunger and satiety cues. This reduces the chances of overeating, too.

Now that you have been introduced to different lifestyle changes that will help tackle stress, there is one thing you need to become mindful of: your environment. Your usual surroundings can be a source of stress. Chances are you never even considered this. So, let's learn what you can do about this external component of stress management.

TAKING CARE OF YOUR
ENVIRONMENT

*M*ental health and the environment you are exposed to are intrinsically related. The places where you spend a lot of your time significantly affect how you feel about yourself and your mental health. This is known as an "environmental factor in psychology. Understanding the different environmental factors and how they affect you makes it easier to see what you can do to feel better.

Simply put, environmental factors affect our mental health. The environment you are used to can increase or reduce your stress levels. Does this make you skeptical? If you take a few minutes and think about the following, you will know the answer yourself.

For instance, cluttered spaces can create feelings of anxiety and overwhelm you. On the other hand, a tidy space can make you feel calmer and more relaxed. Similarly, lighting, temperature, smells, sounds, and the color pallet of the environment you are exposed to determine your comfort levels. For instance, a loud and harshly lit space can trigger agitation. Similarly, dark and cold spaces can leave you unmotivated, especially in a cold winter.

Apart from the physical setting, even those you interact with can be a source of stress. It becomes stressful if you have regular conflicts or miscommunication with people, or unreliable people just surround you. For instance, you might feel comfortable and happy around some people, whereas you may feel extremely uncomfortable and on edge around others.

Another aspect of the environment that can become a source of stress is familiarity. For instance, if a specific setting reminds you of a difficult time in your life, someone toxic, or just disorganization, it can trigger feelings of anxiety. On the other hand, looking at family photos, familiar objects, or keepsakes can improve your mood. This is how powerful your usual environment is. Once you learn to take care of it, your ability to manage stress also improves.

WHERE IS YOUR SAFE SPACE?

What does a safe space mean? This can mean different things to different people. It can refer to an environment where you are safe from physical threats. It could also be a space where you can be authentic without the fear of judgment or criticism. At home, this could refer to a place where you can relax, unwind, and simply be yourself because it offers physical and emotional security. Safe space is needed because it promotes your overall sense of calmness. The idea is to create a little space where you feel safe and secure. If you live with others, talking to them honestly about what you need and your requirements will improve your sense of security. Similarly, you can also block a little time for yourself to be left undisturbed and spend it privately and freely in your space.

ENVIRONMENTAL FACTORS

We are all exposed to different environments daily. From home to work, we are not restricted to a single space. Now, let's try to understand how different environmental factors affect us.

Let's start with your home environment. This is more than a place for physical dwelling. This environment also includes other factors such as the people around you, comprising those you share your home with as well as other community members. Some common home-based environmental factors that can increase your stress are the general climate, pollution levels, social status, and crime levels. For instance, if you live in a high-crime neighborhood, your chances of feeling physically secure in your home are reduced.

Your work environment plays a crucial role in your mental health. Most of the stress we experience these days is often due to our work. For instance, even if you are working hard but don't get any reward for it, there is no social support at the workplace, you are dealing with workplace bullying, or you feel you are not valued or respected at work, it can become a source of stress. If the job comes with plenty of responsibilities and increasing demands, it can further worsen the stress you are experiencing.

Another important environmental factor you must consider is your social environment. This usually includes socioeconomic elements such as social support, race, ethnicity, etc. Though they probably don't sound like much, these elements ultimately shape our usual social environment. It normally includes your friends, family members, acquaintances, and pretty much everyone you come in contact with regularly. It determines and defines your social circle. It has a profound effect on your ability to deal with stress. It is reassuring to know that you have a couple of people you love, trust, and can share intimate details of your life with. This is one of the reasons why any disturbances in personal relationships often increase the stress we experience. It can further be a source of loneliness, isolation, and poor mood. It is important to take stock of your current relationships. Some might uplift you, while others may bring you down. Make more room for all things good in life by moving on from relationships that don't serve you.

CREATING YOUR SAFE SPACE

If you want to create a safe space for yourself, here are some suggestions.

The first aspect you need to concentrate on is physical safety. Privacy can be limited if you live in an apartment complex or an extremely busy neighborhood. The simplest way to ensure physical security is by securing your home. Simple home security tips such as doorbell cameras, screen doors, and study locks will do the trick. You can find a home security solution for pretty much any budget.

Once physical safety is taken care of, focus on emotional safety. This is extremely personal, and everyone has different needs and experiences. Think about whether your home meets your needs or not. For instance, using a weighted blanket might promote sensory comfort at night. Similarly, hanging photos of your loved ones or happy memories where you can often see them can make you feel better. To reduce emotional stress, disconnect from anything that can trigger it. Keeping an area free of all gadgets and technology is a good idea. Usually, ensure the bedroom is the space for this. In the bedroom, avoid watching television or spending time on your phone. Instead, use it only for sleeping. Anything that can disrupt your sleep at night must not be allowed in this room.

Now, it is time to define your safe space. You can only decide what you want to do in this room and what is not allowed. You can also decide who enters. While defining your space, it's not about the size of your sanctuary. It is okay even if it is just a corner in the living room. Instead, it's about thinking about everything you can do to improve your sense of positivity and calmness. Perhaps you want a safe space to be free of any distractions. If so, you can restrict electronics and their use here.

While defining your safe space, you must also focus on aesthetics. Remember, this is your space. You are the only one in control. Therefore, you can decide how you want it to look. The aesthetics are extremely important. For instance, you can opt for a soothing or calming color palette like soft pastels. Investing in an essential oil diffuser is a good idea, too; you can use it to diffuse your favorite calming scents. So, go ahead and plan the aesthetics of your safe space.

Once you have gone through all the steps mentioned until now, your safe space is ready. The next step is to simply start using it daily.

CULTIVATING YOUR ENVIRONMENT

As with every other stress management technique you have been introduced to, you can cultivate a positive environment for yourself. It's quite easy to blame a toxic work environment or a cluttered house for the stress you are experiencing. However, how you perceive the environment sometimes contributes to how you feel. For instance, if you feel you are satisfied with life, this sense of satisfaction will affect how you view everything that happens to you. On the other hand, if you are already feeling a little low and something goes wrong, it can worsen your mood.

If you are in a position where you cannot do anything to change your environment, then reframing your beliefs is the best option available. Find something you appreciate in your immediate environment, even if it is just one good thing, and it will make you feel better. It helps reframe your thoughts about the situation you are in. For instance, creating a habit that helps reduce clutter in your immediate surroundings can make you feel better. If you regularly work at a desk cluttered by old files and things you don't need, you may feel stressed just by looking at it. On the other hand, if the same desk is clean, tidy, and well organized, you will feel better working there. Look for little things you can do to know what works and supports you in the existing environment. You can also add some personal items to spruce up a given space.

When it comes to cultivating a positive environment for yourself, you first need to identify if a change is needed. You must become aware of your feelings and the triggers responsible for them. After this, you can start making small changes wherever possible and necessary to change your current environment. For instance, if city life leaves you feeling overstimulated and anxious, calming activities at home is a good idea. You might not be able to change your workplace, but you can do something to calm yourself at home. Similarly, you might feel better when you get away from the hustle-bustle of city life.

That said, running away from the environment or moving from one to another permanently might not always be an option. In such instances, do whatever you can to make your current setting suit your needs. This isn't a process that can be accomplished overnight. However, with conscious practice and effort, it is possible. Also, if moving away from the existing environment is an option, then go ahead and do it. The best way to regulate stress is to focus on all of the things within your control. If you constantly focus on factors beyond your control, it will make you feel helpless. Instead, you will feel better by shifting your attention to things you can control. Even if it is something as simple as reorganizing your work desk, do it. This will increase your sense of control. At times, this is all that is needed to feel calmer.

The first thing you need to do when you want to improve your environment is to focus on the space you spend most of your time in. Whether it is your bedroom or at work, start there. Keep it functional and free of clutter. If you are working from home, consider setting up a dedicated area. If most of your time is spent in the kitchen, consider reorganizing it and keeping it clean and tidy. This makes a lot of difference.

Along with your physical environment, pay attention to your social environment. This means you must pay attention to the different relationships you entertain. We sometimes tend to hold on too tightly to relationships that don't do us any good. Whether it is a toxic friend, co-worker, or family member, learn to sever ties with those constantly bringing you down. Remember, if your life is cluttered with undesirable things, there won't be any space for anything positive. This is true mentally and physically.

STEP 11: ASSESS YOUR CURRENT ENVIRONMENT AND MAKE CHANGES

Until now, you have been introduced to different ways your usual environment and social circle affect you. They can either be a source of positivity or a source of immense stress. The good news is that, as with all the other aspects of stress management you were introduced to until now, even this is in your control. The first step toward making a change is becoming aware of your environment. If you aren't sure how to do this, here are some questions you can answer.

- Who are the five people you spend most of your time with? Do their values align with yours?
- How do you feel around your social circle (including friends and family)?
- Are you tired, drained, or just low after meeting certain people? Who are they?

Answering these questions takes a little self-introspection. Sometimes, even those we are close to aren't good for our mental or emotional health. Toxic relationships aren't worth holding on to. They will simply become a source of your stress or worsen it. Once you identify the positive and toxic relationships in your life, the next step is to focus on the good and eliminate the undesirable.

This brings us to the end of the 11-step approach to tackling stress. Even though the steps are different, they are all equally important. The next step is to implement everything you have been introduced to into your daily life. Doing this will better prepare you for any curve balls that life throws your way. You will need to incorporate these 11 steps for better stress management and ensure you stick to them as well. With a little conscious effort, commitment, persistence, and patience, you can truly tackle stress. You can enjoy the peaceful and joyful life you desire. You are the writer of your destiny, and now, it's time to get started.

We hope you enjoyed Stress Less & Live Again. Please take a minute to place an Amazon review by scanning this QR code or by searching Amazon for the book. Thank you!

AFTERWORD

Unsurprisingly, stress is on the rise, especially chronic stress. We all seem to be struggling with one problem or another. The list goes on, whether it is financial problems, personal issues, career-related problems, midlife crises, or health problems. The list of problems most of us face is pretty much endless in today's world.

We all get stressed from time to time. There is nothing wrong with a little stress in regulated amounts. It can act as a motivator to help get things done. Whether it is preparing for an important presentation at work or making a conscious effort to improve your relationships, a little stress is good. However, it becomes problematic when stress becomes our constant companion, and in the modern world, we seem to be bombarded by stressors wherever we look.

If you constantly feel like your life has become an uphill battle, the walls are closing in with no way out, or you struggle in every aspect of your life, it is a sign of chronic stress. Chronic stress occurs when your normal stress response doesn't subside even after eliminating the stressor.

Since there are different stressors, we all respond differently to them. Regardless of what is causing your stress, its signs are almost always the same. You were introduced to an 11-step approach to tackling stress in this book.

The first step toward tackling stress is awareness. You need to first become aware that you are stressed, and only then can you take corrective action. Once you have become aware of the fact that you are stressed, the next step is to identify what is causing your stress. You can identify your stress triggers by understanding them through the simple and practical activities given in this book.

Your job doesn't end here, though. Instead, the next step to tackle stress is understanding your existing coping mechanisms. Since the causes of stress are different, we deal with them differently, too. Some mechanisms are healthy, whereas others are unhealthy. By learning to identify your existing coping mechanisms, it becomes easier to determine whether they are helping or hindering your ability to deal with stress.

After awareness comes acceptance. Unless you accept that you are stressed, you cannot make the changes needed to change your situation. A common problem most of us face is we struggle to ask for help. Using the different suggestions in this book, you can effectively take the fourth step to manage stress—asking for help. Whether you are reaching out to your loved ones or a professional, go ahead and do it. The benefits of obtaining the help you need are innumerable. So, don't hesitate and reach out whenever you need.

Simply becoming aware and accepting the fact that you are stressed does not solve your problem, though. Even if you know your coping mechanisms, understand that there is always an opportunity to develop healthier habits to tackle stress. Using the suggestions given in this book, you can take the fifth step to tackle stress, which is building new habits. By focusing on habits that are easy to implement and practicing them, your ability to tackle stress improves.

Even though stress causes various physical symptoms, it all starts in the mind. Your mind is the most powerful tool to face stress head-on. You can shift your attitude and mindset by learning to regulate your thoughts, shifting from negative to positive thinking, and making positive affirmations a part of your life. A simple change will make you feel more in control of your life and yourself. This, in turn, helps tackle stress. This is the sixth step of managing stress.

Most of us lead hectic lives. It might feel as if we have no time to unwind or destress. In such instances, the best thing you can do is simply slow down; this is the seventh step. Pause, meditate, journal, and learn to appreciate the simple things in life. Practicing gratitude and slowing down makes it easier to regulate your stress and life.

Now that you have taken the seventh step to tackle stress, the eighth one is to focus on making healthier lifestyle changes. The simplest change you can make is to prioritize quality sleep. When your body and mind get the rest they need, they function effectively and efficiently. This, in turn, makes it easier to tackle stress.

Apart from focusing on sleep, another healthy change you must make is to incorporate exercise into your daily life. Whether it is playing a sport you enjoy, going to the gym, or doing something else that gets your body moving, go ahead and do it. Even if it is just for 20 minutes daily, ensure you exercise regularly. This will automatically improve your physical, mental, and emotional well-being. When you are stronger on all these fronts, managing stress also becomes easier.

Don't forget to focus on the food you are consuming, too. After all, what you eat sustains your body and mind. Therefore, shifting to a healthier diet, eliminating stress-related eating, and becoming mindful of what you eat will nourish your body and mind. It will also further enhance your relationship with food. A combination of these factors will make you feel better.

And finally, the eleventh step to tackling stress is to focus on your usual environment. If your environment is not conducive to healthy and stress-free living, tackling stress becomes challenging. Using the different suggestions in this book, you can create a healthier and safer environment in all aspects of your life. So, keeping stress at bay is a perfectly achievable and sustainable goal using the suggestions and advice given in this book.

Life's curveballs come in the least expected moments, and there will be days where you feel like you can no longer push through—but don't give up! It's true each day will never be the same, but with this book beside you, you can always find the strength to push through, overcome stress, and live life with joy and peace. So, what are you waiting for? Take the first step toward managing stress by implementing the advice given in this book.

Before you go, I have a small favor to ask. If you enjoyed reading this book and found it informative, please spare a few minutes to leave a review on Amazon. Thank you, and all the best!

BIBLIOGRAPHY

Ackerman, C. (2019, July 10). *83 Benefits of journaling for depression, anxiety, and stress*. Positive Psychology. https://positivepsychology.com/benefits-of-journaling/

American Addiction Centers. (2019, June 13). *Addiction as a coping mechanism and healthy alternatives*. American Addiction Centers. https://americanaddictioncenters.org/sobriety-guide/coping-mechanism

American Heart Association. (2021, September 13). *Elevated stress hormones linked to higher risk of high blood pressure and heart events*. Science Daily. https://www.sciencedaily.com/releases/2021/09/210913135723.htm

American Psychological Association. (2021). *Manage stress: Strengthen your support network*. APA. https://www.apa.org/topics/stress/manage-social-support

American Association for Marriage and Family Therapy. (2019). *Substance abuse and intimate relationships*. Aamft. https://www.aamft.org/Consumer_Updates/Substance_Abuse_and_Intimate_Relationships.aspx

American Psychological Association. (2021). *What's the difference between stress and anxiety?* Apa. https://www.apa.org/topics/stress/anxiety-difference

Banner Health. (2022, March 10). *How to tell the difference between good and bad stress | banner*. Bannerhealth. https://www.bannerhealth.com/healthcareblog/teach-me/bad-stress-vs-good-stress-how-can-i-tell-the-difference

Batson, J. (2011). *What is stress?* The American Institute of Stress. https://www.stress.org/daily-life

Clear, J. (2013, May 13). *How to break a bad habit (and replace it with a good one)*. James Clear. https://jamesclear.com/how-to-break-a-bad-habit

Clear, J. (2015). *How to master the art of continuous improvement*. James Clear. https://jamesclear.com/continuous-improvement

Cleveland Clinic. (2021, June 15). *Eat these foods to reduce stress and anxiety*. Health Essentials from Cleveland Clinic. https://health.clevelandclinic.org/eat-these-foods-to-reduce-stress-and-anxiety/

Cleveland Clinic. (2021, January 28). *What is stress? symptoms, signs & more.*

Cleveland Clinic. https://my.clevelandclinic.org/health/articles/11874-stress

Cronkleton, E. (2021, May 4). *Yoga for stress: Breath, poses, and meditation to calm anxiety.* Healthline. https://www.healthline.com/health/fitness/yoga-for-stress

Davidson, K. (2020, December 3). *Five tips for developing a better relationship with food.* Healthline. https://www.healthline.com/nutrition/fixing-a-bad-relationship-with-food

Eatough, E. (2022, August 18). *Here's how identifying your stress triggers can help you to relax.* Betterup. https://www.betterup.com/blog/stress-triggers

Elizabeth, D. (2021, August 21). *Using your internal narrative for a happier life – Wild simple joy.* Wild Simple Joy. https://wildsimplejoy.com/internal-narrative/

Harvard Health Publishing. (2020, July 7). *Exercising to relax.* Harvard Health. https://www.health.harvard.edu/staying-healthy/exercising-to-relax

Harvard School of Public Health. (2020, October 5). *Stress and health.* The Nutrition Source. https://www.hsph.harvard.edu/nutrition-source/stress-and-health/

Heffer, T., & Willoughby, T. (2017). A count of coping strategies: A longitudinal study investigating an alternative method to understanding coping and adjustment. *PLOS ONE, 12*(10), e0186057. https://doi.org/10.1371/journal.pone.0186057

How to Recognize the Causes of Stress. (2020, March 29). Healthline. https://www.healthline.com/health/stress-causes#:~:text=Identifying%20the%20causes%20of%20stress

Hunter-Bailey, L. (2021, February 5). *Five benefits you'll gain from cutting off toxic "friends."* Wholistique. https://medium.com/wholistique/5-benefits-youll-gain-from-cutting-off-toxic-friends-49d931f493bb

Johnson, J. (2018, September 5). *Stress and sleep: What's the link?* Medical-newstoday. https://www.medicalnewstoday.com/articles/322994

Kandola, A., & Sharon, A. (2022, January 3). *Chronic stress: Symptoms, health effects, and how to manage it.* Medicalnewstoday. https://www.medical-newstoday.com/articles/323324#chronic-stress

Kennedy, K. (2019, March 26). *The 10 best foods to help fight stress.* Everyday-Health. https://www.everydayhealth.com/diet-nutrition-pictures/how-to-reduce-stress-with-diet.aspx

Lindberg, S. (2023, March 23). *How your environment affects your mental health.* Verywell Mind. https://www.verywellmind.com/hoWw-your-environment-affects-your-mental-health-5093687

Madell, R. (2012). *Exercise as stress relief.* Healthline Media. https://www.healthline.com/health/heart-disease/exercise-stress-relief

Mayo Clinic Staff. (2020, April 22). *Meditation: A simple, fast way to reduce stress.* Mayo Clinic. https://www.mayoclinic.org/tests-procedures/meditation/in-depth/meditation/art-20045858

Mental Health Foundation. (2018). *Stress: statistics.* Mental Health. https://www.mentalhealth.org.uk/explore-mental-health/mental-health-statistics/stress-statistics

Raypole, C. (2020, August 18). *Mantra meditation: Benefits, how to try it, and more.* Healthline. https://www.healthline.com/health/mantra-meditation

Raypole, C. (2020, August 27). *Eight ways to actually enjoy the little things.* Healthline. https://www.healthline.com/health/enjoy-the-little-things

Rekhi, S. (n.d.). *Coping mechanisms: Definition, examples, & types.* The Berkeley Well-Being Institute. https://www.berkeleywellbeing.com/coping-mechanisms.html

Robinson, L., Segal, J., & Smith, M. (2018). *How to start exercising and stick to it: Making exercise an enjoyable part of your everyday life.* Helpguide. https://www.helpguide.org/articles/healthy-living/how-to-start-exercising-and-stick-to-it.htm

Sinha, R. (2008). Chronic Stress, Drug Use, and Vulnerability to Addiction. *Annals of the New York Academy of Sciences, 1141*(1), 105–130. https://doi.org/10.1196/annals.1441.030

Smith, K. (2022, January 6). *Is social media busting or boosting your stress?* EverydayHealth. https://www.everydayhealth.com/wellness/united-states-of-stress/social-media-busting-boosting-your-stress/

Steven Pressfield Quotes. (n.d.). BrainyQuote. https://www.brainyquote.com/quotes/steven_pressfield_528008

Strong, R. (2022, September 19). *Your habits matter more than you might think —Here's why.* Healthline. https://www.healthline.com/health/mental-health/why-are-habits-important

Viktor, V. (2022, September 2). *Twenty-five signs to tell fake friends from real friends.* SocialSelf. https://socialself.com/blog/fake-friends/

Vinall, M. (2021, March 11). *Mantras for anxiety: Harness the healing power of chanting to ease fear, stress, and depression.* Healthline. https://www.healthline.com/health/mind-body/mantras-for-anxiety#benefits

Villines, Z. (2022, May 23). *Mantras for anxiety: Types, benefits, and more.* Medicalnewstoday. https://www.medicalnewstoday.com/articles/mantras-for-anxiety#for-anxiety

Wolfers, L. N., & Utz, S. (2022). Social media use, stress, and coping. *Current Opinion in Psychology, 45*(101305), 101305. https://doi.org/10.1016/j.copsyc.2022.101305

World Health Organization. (2023, February 21). *Stress.* World Health Organization. https://www.who.int/news-room/questions-and-answers/item/stress#:~:text=Stress%20can%20be%20defined%20as

Yeun, C. (2020, May 12). *How to fall asleep in 10, 60, or 120 seconds.* Healthline. https://www.healthline.com/health/healthy-sleep/fall-asleep-fast

Zelman, K. M. (2008). *10 Tips for finding the best diet that works for you.* WebMD. https://www.webmd.com/diet/features/ten-tips-for-finding-the-best-diet-that-works-for-you

19282092R00080